B51 072 88

D0718689

The Boy Who Wanted to Fly

ROTHERHAM LIBRARY SERVICE	
B512880	
Bertrams	17/01/2011
AN	£7.99
CLS	361.7409

The Boy Who Wanted to Fly

Don Mullan

Legend Press

Independent Book Publisher

Legend Press Ltd, 2 London Wall Buildings,
London EC2M 5UU
info@legend-paperbooks.co.uk
www.legendpress.co.uk
www.twitter.com/legend_press

Contents © Don Mullan 2010

First Published 2006 under title 'A Hero Who Could Fly'

The right of the above author to be identified as the author of
this work has been asserted by them in accordance with the
Copyright, Designs and Patent Act 1988.

British Library Cataloguing in Publication Data available.

ISBN 978-1-9077560-1-6

Set in Times
Printed by J F Print Ltd., Sparkford, Somerset.

Cover designed by Tim Bremner

All rights reserved. No part of this publication may be
reproduced, stored in or introduced into a retrieval system, or trans-
mitted, in any form, or by any means electronic, mechanical, photo-
copying, recording or otherwise, without the prior permission of the
publisher. Any person who commits any unauthorised act in relation
to this publication may be liable to criminal prosecution
and civil claims for damages.

Legend 📖 Press
Independent Book Publisher

Contents

Don Mullan

Don Mullan was born in Derry in 1956. As a schoolboy, his boyhood hero was the great England goalkeeper, Gordon Banks.

Mullan witnessed Bloody Sunday at the age of fifteen. His involvement with the Northern Ireland Civil Rights movement led to work on civil and human rights issues around the world. In 1980, he became Director of AFrI (Action From Ireland), a Dublin-based justice, peace and human rights organisation. Later, he worked as a volunteer in Brazil, and spent two years with Concern Worldwide.

In 1993 Mullan learnt that he is dyslexic but pursued a career as writer and investigative journalist. His book *Eyewitness Bloody Sunday* was a catalyst for re-opening the public inquiry in 1998, and inspired the award-winning movie, *Bloody Sunday*. In 2002, he received the 'Defenders of Human Dignity Award' from the International League for Human Rights at the United Nations.

Mullan is currently creating a number of projects related to the theme of Sport for Development and Peace. This includes the creation of a Flanders Peace Field, inspired by the remarkable 1914 Christmas Truce on the Western Front during which German and British soldiers played a game of football.

Also by the Author

Eyewitness Bloody Sunday – The Truth (Wolfhound Press, 1997, Roberts Rinehart Publishers Inc, USA 1997; 2nd Ed. Merlin Books, 2002)

The Dublin and Monaghan Bombings – The Truth, The Questions and the Victims' Stories (Wolfhound Press, 2000)

A Gift of Roses (Wolfhound Press, 2001)

Contacted with co-author Audrey Healy (Mercier Press, 2005)

Speaking Truth to Power: The Donal De Roiste Affair (Currach Books, 2006)

The 'Little Book' Series (Columba Press, Dublin): 12 titles to-date including:
A Little Book of St. Francis of Assisi (2002)
A Little Book of Mother Teresa of Calcutta (2003)
A Little Book of St. Patrick (2004)

To
The Memory of My Father
and
John ('Our Jack') Banks
and to
Todd Allen, an American friend, whose support, generosity
and trust made it possible for us to launch the Gordon
Banks Monument Project.

Foreword

By Pelé and
Archbishop Desmond Tutu

Gordon Banks and Don Mullan were the reason we met for the first time in 2008 in England.

Banks, one of the greatest goalkeepers in the history of football, and Mullan, who, as an Irish boy, found inspiration and hope in his English hero.

Don Mullan's boyhood memoir is a heart-warming and moving story. The first ten years of his life are filled with a great deal of confusion and doubt because of undiagnosed dyslexia that many adults, including teachers, believed was due to a low IQ.

The gift of life, however, is laced with moments of serendipity that have the ability to change our course in profound and dynamic ways. And that's what happened the day Don saw Gordon Banks play for England in the 1966 World Cup Final.

Saturday 30 July, 1966 was not only a momentous day for the English and their eleven heroes who lifted the Jules Rimet trophy at Wembley. Unexpectedly, it also proved to be for a young Irish boy living in a working class area of Northern Ireland that was soon to be plunged into turbulence and war. It was as though a door opened in his mind, allowing fresh air and light to dispel the fog of confusion and doubt that had nestled there from his first day at school. Suddenly the Irish boy had a hero – an English hero – who inspired him to excel and who motivated him to become a respected schoolboy goalkeeper.

Like millions of boys around the globe, Don's ambition was to become a professional footballer like Banks and, one day, play for his country. And, like millions of such boys, that never happened for various reasons. But the friendships he made and the discipline he learned from the game ultimately helped to form Don's character and make him a better person. And that is the greatest result sport can hope to achieve. At all levels, sport should not be about winning at any cost. Its primary goal should be about helping young people to become better, more healthy and caring citizens. That goal is far more important than winning medals, even World Cup and Olympic medals.

And, thankfully, that's what sport did for Don Mullan.

The outbreak of the Northern Ireland 'Troubles' in 1968 posed new challenges to Don's development as a teenager. He was a close witness to many seminal events in the Northern Ireland conflict, including, in 1972, the tragedy of Bloody Sunday. That event alone was to fuel national bitterness and hatred for more than a quarter of a century.

Yet Don credits a meeting with Gordon Banks, just 18 months earlier, as a calming influence that helped him choose the way of peace over violence.

Gordon Banks, of course, was oblivious to all of this until

an evening in March 2005 when the boy he met in 1970 met him again as an adult. Don brought with him his treasured boyhood scrapbook that we ourselves have had the joy of seeing and signing. The word 'scrapbook' diminishes what it actually is. It is a giant 500-page wallpaper book into which a young dyslexic boy lovingly gathered every picture and piece of written information he could find on his hero. We can state without fear of contradiction, it has to be one of the greatest and most moving tributes a child – anywhere in the world – has created to a hero. The time, the dedication, the focus, determination and absolute love that went into every page is evident with each turning.

And it was that love, expressed as gratitude, that motivated the boy to create a statue to Gordon Banks in 2008, which we were to have the honour of unveiling.

We both travelled across the globe to be part of a wonderful day of celebration that was as much about the ten-year-old boy as it was about his English football hero.

And Don Mullan's choice of a hero was well made. Gordon Banks is not just a sporting legend; he is first and foremost a generous, caring and humble human being with a beautiful family. It was, indeed, our great privilege to unveil a monument that will immortalise his memory for generations to come.

We are reminded of Antoine de Saint-Exupòry's *The Little Prince* and the core nugget of wisdom his novel contains:

… it is only with the heart that one can see rightly, what is essential is invisible to the eye.

This is a book to be encountered by the heart.

We hope the readers of this boyhood memoir find the same joy and inspiration we too found in it. For sport is not just about what happens on the field of play. It is also what happens beyond and through it. And an integral part of all sport is its fans.

This book is written by a fan who has retained a lifelong love for sport and a growing realisation of its positive role in his journey from schoolboy goalkeeper to a global citizen with friends in Asia, Africa, Europe and the Americas. That realisation is primarily focused on his boyhood hero – and now friend – Gordon Banks. This book is written with gratitude for all that Gordon Banks inspired within him as a boy and a youth, often in difficult and challenging circumstances. And the day we all met in Stoke-on-Trent in 2008 for the unveiling of the first-phase of a monument to Gordon Banks, was the culmination of the Irish boy's gratitude for his English hero. It is a project not yet completed, as Don describes in his postscript. But we are certain that many people of goodwill and generosity, who see the beauty of this story with their hearts, will help *The Boy Who Wanted To Fly* complete his dream.

Given the history of Ireland and England, this is a story and a friendship that all sport, and football in particular, should celebrate. Enjoy!

+ Desmond M Tutu   **Edson Arantes do Nascimento**
Archbishop Emeritus   **Pelé**
South Africa   **Brazil**

Foreword by Gabriel Byrne

From the original edition

1970. It is a moment made immortal. A confluence of instinct, skill, luck, daring. A frozen moment of poetry, Gordon Banks in mid-air, impossibly flicking that perfect header from Pelé over the bar – the greatest save he'd ever seen, said the Brazilian. And in a crowded pub in Dublin, as we watched on a black and white Bush TV, breath stilled, we knew we'd never forget…

This story is about Gordon Banks and another hero – Don Mullan's working class father, a warehouseman, who could never have known the powerful influence the meeting he arranged with Banksy would have on his awestruck dyslexic youngest son. Whether we believe in destiny or not, that fateful moment changed a boy forever, inspiring him – with hope and imagination. Don's work as an investigative journalist and humanitarian stands in its own way as a guiding light and inspiration for those who would aspire to a better world.

Gabriel Byrne,
New York , March 2006

1

My Father

After the 1966 World Cup Final – the first live game of soccer I watched on TV – Gordon Banks became my hero and the sole subject of my first book, a giant 500-page scrapbook that I cherish to this day. In 1970, two months after 'That Save' against Pelé in Mexico, Gordon Banks met my father and together they brought magic into my life.

My father died on 12 August 1987, aged sixty-nine. Our family had been keeping vigil with him for several days at Altnagelvin Hospital, Derry. At around 11 o'clock that morning I had just relieved my mother and eldest sister, Moya, and was sitting alone with him in a small, single room. He was drifting in and out of consciousness, occasionally muttering to himself.

At one point I thought I heard him say, "I let yous down." (Yous being a Derry colloquialism that pluralized the word 'you' to include his wife and five children.)

I was shocked and puzzled by the statement and I asked him to repeat it. When he did, I asked him what he meant.

"I never had a good job or home for your mother or yous."

My father was a good man. He had, like many of his generation, only an elementary education. Despite this, I seldom recall him being unemployed and, if he was, he was always busy haggling for work. He spent most of his working life as a labourer and storekeeper. In later years he served alongside his younger brother Paul, an electrician, as a sparks mate and finally worked in my brother Liam's 'Automotive Supplies' shop. He had worked hard to ensure we were never hungry and without.

Our home, a terraced house at 41 Leenan Gardens on the sprawling Creggan Estate, Derry, was generally a happy and loving abode. He and my mother, believing that a trade or a good education would provide their children with the opportunity to escape the poverty trap, made many sacrifices so that we might advance.

On hearing his comments, I immediately left his bedside and went to my four siblings gathered outside: Moya, Liam, Cathal and Deirdre. I told them what he had just uttered. We gathered around his bed and, one by one, affirmed our old man, thanking him for all that he was – and that he meant to us.

Far from being a failure, he was a dedicated father and, like many 'ordinary' working class folk, he was unassuming and humble. We are proud to be his offspring.

To this day I thank God I heard those lamentable words uttered with less than half a day of his life remaining. It would indeed have been a tragedy if my father had died feeling he had failed us; simply because we didn't own our family home or because he didn't have a 'respectable' blue-collar job.

A few days earlier, I had sat through the night with him

in that same room. He awoke during that long hour when the earth seems to have stopped rotating. We began to reminisce. I asked what his happiest memory of me was. I was surprised when he told me it was the night he took me to the local cinema to see *The Magnificent Seven*. I remembered that night vividly, a boy of about six, sitting beside him in the now demolished City Cinema, William Street, my eyes agog at this new wonderland of giant Technicolor cowboy heroes and villains. He recalled my innocent excitement and how I appeared to live every moment.

Then, in this beautiful intimate moment that working-class fathers and sons seldom have, he asked me what mine was of him. There were many to choose from. But one outshone all others.

"The day you brought me to meet Gordon Banks." I told him.

"Yes," he replied, a big smile dawning on his memory of it. "That was a great day. He was a very nice young man. Wasn't he?"

"He sure was," I replied. "He was my boyhood hero."

"I know!" he responded. "Wasn't he amazing? That man could fly. If anyone deserved to meet him, it was you."

I walked to the window to hide my tears. "That man could fly!" What an apt and inspiring description, I thought. And because of Gordon Banks, I was the boy who wanted to fly.

Dawn was breaking over the patchwork quilt of fields and hedgerows that blanketed the hushed foothills of the Sperrin Mountains.

We had made it through another long night.

2

How it all began: The 1966 World Cup

I could never have had a better sporting idol than Gordon Banks. As a boy I modelled my game on him, even the unique way he tossed the ball from his hands and volleyed it with great accuracy into the opposition half.

I come from a working class background in what was one of Northern Ireland's most troubled areas, the Creggan Estate, Derry. Unknown then to myself and my parents was the fact that I am dyslexic, something I discovered much later in 1994, at the age of thirty-eight. My memories of a dyslexic childhood are filled with feelings of low self-esteem, crippling self-doubt and poor co-ordination.

The 1966 England World Cup tournament was televised, thus allowing many youngsters to see in action great soccer stars like England's Jimmy Greaves and Bobby Moore, Portugal's Eusebio and Brazil's Pelé. Wanting to imitate them after each game we'd gather by a low wall beside the field that lay between Leenan and Melmore Gardens. The two best players would pick their teams in descending order of perceived skills. The two boys left sitting on the wall had only one option: goalkeeper. And that's how it all began.

I was ten-years-old. The World Cup Final at Wembley between England and West Germany was on Saturday 30 July 1966. It was the first full game of live soccer I saw on television and I can remember exactly where: at my Uncle Eddie and Auntie Rosaleen's home in the Creggan Estate. I watched it with my cousins Damien and Gerard McLaughlin on their black and white television set. That was the day Gordon Banks began to capture my imagination.

It was a game full of drama and suspense – and controversy. West Germany silenced England's supporters by punishing an early and uncharacteristic defensive error by Ray Wilson, who, off balance, headed a cross to the feet of Helmut Haller. From 15 yards the German midfielder sneaked the ball past Gordon Banks.

BBC commentator, Kenneth Wolstenholm, kept hopes alive with the words, "This is the fourth World Cup Final I've seen and the team that scored first – lost!" Then the stadium was ecstatic six minutes later when Geoff Hurst scored the first of his historic Cup Final hat-trick when he headed a Bobby Moore free kick past the German keeper Hans Tilkowski.

Before the end of the first half Banks pulled off three fine saves. The first was in the 27th minute when Uwe Seller pushed a long ball through the middle to Haller. Spotting the danger Banks was immediately off his line and smothered the ball at his feet. In the 38th minute, Siegfrield Held sent in a low driven corner kick which, despite being sandwiched by Bobby Moore and Nobby Stiles on the near edge of the six yard box, Lothar Emmerich directed out to

Wolfgang Overath, who was positioned where the semi-circle meets the 18-yard box. His low powerful volley brought out a spectacular reflex parry from Banks. The ball fell for Emmerich who, under pressure from Martin Peters and George Cohen, managed only to stab the ball goal-wards and Banks comfortably gathered. Wolstenholm exclaimed, "Well done Gordon Banks – the hero of England!" I was captivated.

In the 42nd minute Uwe Seller carried the ball from the halfway line and, 22 yards out, struck a perfect shot that was sailing towards the top left-hand corner of goal before Banks took flight to tip it over the bar.

Through the second half Banks dealt with everything that came his way. His timing on two high punches was superb. The players, with the apparent exception of Alan Ball, began to tire on the Wembley turf, heavy after two days of rain as divots peppered the pitch.

England was coping better and it was Tilkowski who had to make some important saves as the host nation pressed for a winner. Bobby Moore was marshalling his troops and exhorting everyone to keep focused and calm. With twelve minutes to go, Martin Peter's blasted England into the lead from a Geoff Hurst rebound. Gordon Banks ran the length of Wembley to congratulate him. That was the first time Germany had conceded two goals in a World Cup match.

With eight minutes to go Bobby Moore passed the ball back to Ray Wilson, who started a chain reaction back to Jack Charlton and Banks. The fans booed and whistled the time-wasting, then began to chant, "We want three!"

With only a minute to go and the whole of England set to celebrate the ultimate achievement in the game it had invented, West Germany pulled off a Houdini escape from a free-kick awarded, unfairly, against big Jack Charlton. Lothar Emmerich sent the ball towards the right edge of the England six-yard box, which Cohen only managed to half-stop. The West German defender, Wolfgang Weber, raced onto a Siegfried Held pass and thundered the ball just inside the left upright.

English players, including Banks, protested, claiming that Karl-Heinz Schnellinger had handled the ball on its way to Held, but Swiss referee Gottfried Dienst brushed aside their remonstrations, and a few seconds later the final was to go into extra time. Banks famously likened the West German equaliser to "... being pushed off Everest with just a stride to go to the top."

Then most controversial goal of the game and, unquestionably, in World Cup history – Geoff Hurst's second goal, and England's third, ten minutes into extra time. Alan Ball sent in a cross from the right wing, which Hurst thundered against the underside of the German crossbar. The ball lunged earthwards and to this day the awarded goal is disputed. Did it cross the line or not? Referee Dienst, after consulting his Russian linesman, Tofik Bakhramov decided. It was a goal! The score: 3-2.

Confusion reigned in the dying minute as some England fans began to invade the pitch. Wolstenholm's commentary told it all: "And here comes Hurst, he's got... [seeing the invading fans] ... some people are on the pitch, they think it's all over. [Hurst shoots – and scores his hat-trick] ... It is now! And it's four"!

Everest was conquered and England collected the Jules Rimet trophy from the Royal Box.

In an interview in Dortmund for this book, the 1966 West German goalkeeper, Hans Tilkowski, was adamant that the Swiss referee and Russian linesman had robbed his team. During the interview I was explaining 'hat-trick' to my German-English translator, Annegret Kopp, as she was unfamiliar with the term. When I said Geoff Hurst was the first and only player to have scored three goals in a World Cup Final, Tilkowski firmly corrected me, "No! One goal." He raised his right index finger to emphasise the point and then proceed to laugh heartily.

Tilkowski said that he touched Geoff Hurst's shot on its way to the underside of the crossbar. "I then saw it bounce on the goal line and I am certain it never crossed the line!" He was critical of the Russian linesman, sketching for me the acute angle the linesman was standing at – thus making it impossible to see clearly. "To make a sound determination," Tilkowski argued, "the linesman would have had to be standing on the back line, at the corner post. He wasn't!"

He also said there was confusion at the end of the game when the referee blew his whistle, causing fans to invade the pitch. He says that the referee should have stopped the game at that moment to remove the fans but he didn't, and it was then that Hurst scored his third.

I liked Hans Tilkowski. He came across as a kind and caring man. He told me that the style of goalkeeping he admired most was best found in Lev Yashin, Bert Trautmann and Gordon Banks. He told me he remains very friendly with Banks and many of the 1966 England team. He now works as a goodwill ambassador for a humanitarian organisation and spends much of his time helping charities dealing with cystic fibrosis, multiple sclerosis and children suffering from cancer.

"Naturally, the 1966 World Cup Final was a disappointment to me personally," he told me, "but it was only a game. It is more important that as footballers we try to use our influence to create a better world. I hope that during the 40th anniversary, the England and German teams of 1966 are brought together to celebrate friendship and sportsmanship as an example of the kind of values the game of soccer and the world needs today."

With the final whistle deserted English streets thronged with jubilant fans and a national carnival ensued. The eleven English heroes were destined for immortality in the eyes of the people.

Response to their victory was more subdued back in Derry, but I don't remember resentment. My older cousin Damien, a football enthusiast, was very pleased. I knew that something special had just happened for the English. Soon after, when I started my Gordon Banks scrapbook, I sellotaped into its opening pages an account of England's victorious 1966 campaign, neatly copied in my 10-year-old handwriting.

Neither history nor politics impinged on me then. I wore a yellow goalkeeper's jersey and found a crest with three lions, which my mother sewed on. Thus, when I turned out for my street soccer team, I was the England goalkeeper!

I practised, practised, practised. My game began to improve and eventually the boys in the street realised that a good goalkeeper was equal to a good striker. From being a very timid child, through goalkeeping, I discovered a talent and an identity.

3

The Scrapbook

Dyslexic children need an interest to help them sustain and develop their reading skills and every picture, article and drawing I could find on Gordon Banks was carefully cut out and sellotaped into an old wallpaper book. It was given to me by Tom and Jim Canning, who owned a local paint and decorating shop. To this day, my Gordon Banks scrapbook is a treasured possession. This was also my first major piece of investigative journalism!

My parents had the wisdom to recognise that something very healthy had begun in my life. I was playing sport and also developing my intellectual skills. While I wasn't able to read Shakespeare or James Joyce, what I was doing would, in time, help me to do so.

I used to go to the local library at Brook Park and head for the sports section to check out the latest soccer books. I'm embarrassed to admit it but, if I found a picture of Banksy in a book, I pretended to be reading it while carefully removing the photograph for my scrapbook. A few years later the library was blown up by the IRA and all the books destroyed, so I smile now whenever I come across those few pages of Gordon Banks that I saved.

At the end of every football match, win or lose, I would go and shake the hand of our opposition players and thank them for the game. Why? Because that's what Gordon Banks did. He was a down-to-earth, respectful, fair-minded and sporting professional. I consider myself the luckiest boy in the world to have discovered a supreme sportsman in every sense.

Nowadays there is a growing cynicism about the game of football, especially when we see the antics of some fat cats who have lost all sense of perspective. The English Football Association have made a huge error in failing to utilise men of immense character like Gordon Banks. The same applies to some football clubs and local authorities.

The professionals' modesty and decency are what the game needs today, for players and fans. I was saddened when I learned that Gordon decided to sell his 1966 world cup winner's medal and cap in 2001. It is shameful that the English Football Association does not make use of the towering legends of 1966 as ambassadors of values that were once crucial, and which need to be urgently rediscovered on and off the pitch.

Banksy Mullan

The following year, inspired by the Black civil rights movement in the USA, the Northern Ireland Civil Rights Movement was founded, primarily to campaign for Catholic rights. On the 5 October 1968, RUC officers attacked peaceful demonstrators during a Civil Rights march in my hometown of Derry. As I looked at pictures of the police cracking open heads and emptying lungs of air, I asked 'Why?'

It was the first political question I ever asked. I was twelve-years-old.

Following unrelenting street disturbances in August 1969, the British Army were ordered onto the streets of Belfast and Derry. In the early days they engaged in various community liaison projects. It was not unusual for local clubs to play games against regimental teams.

I also recall on one occasion a British Army band, I think Royal Marines, coming to our school. We gave them a rapturous welcome, preferring their brass and percussion instruments to English, Maths and French. Our school was the first in Northern Ireland to be offered an Adventure Training Course by the army for which there were only ten or twelve places. I was the school under-13 and under-15 goalkeeper and, because of my dedication to training, the PE teachers, headed by Mr. Charlie Fisher, gave me the opportunity.

It was a boyhood epic which included rock climbing, hill walking, canoeing, orienteering and expedition work in early May 1970, less than a month before the Mexico World Cup. Our base was Magilligan Camp, about 25 miles from Derry, which later became a detention centre for internees in August 1971 and the theatre for an ominous encounter between unarmed Civil Rights demonstrators and 1 Para the week before Bloody Sunday, 1972.

But those developments lay in the unknown future. Then, the exciting summer evenings at Magilligan Camp often finished with a game of football and it was there the

British Army gave me the nickname 'Banksy Mullan' because of my talkative enthusiasm for the art of goalkeeping, and my hero, Gordon Banks.

4

Mexico 1970: That Save

There was some additional excitement in Derry as the World Cup approached. In March, Ireland won the 1970 Eurovision Song Contest for the first time with *All Kinds of Everything* sung by Rosemary Brown (Dana), a teenager from Creggan

On the day Dana topped the British charts, a young Derry songwriter and composer, Phil Coulter, who had already helped the UK to 1st and 2nd places in the 1967 and 1968 contests with *Puppet on a String* and *Congratulations*, re-entered the British charts along with the England World Cup Squad. Coulter teamed up with Bill Martin to write the single *Back Home* and produce an LP called *The World Beaters Sing The World Beaters*.

On 16th May 1970, two weeks before England's opening game with Romania, *Back Home* hit number one, revealed on *Top of the Pops*, remaining there for three weeks. The song was in the British charts for 17 weeks and remains the most successful ever written to accompany the England team into a World or European tournament. *The World Beaters Sing The World Beaters*, entered the album charts on 16th May and remained there for eight weeks, reaching the number four spot.

I copied the words of the song on a school writing pad that I tore out and sellotaped onto page 281 of my scrapbook. I wrote the following note (spelt as it was written!):

Before the 1970 World Cup Finals in Mexico, Gordon Banks appeared with the rest of his England Team Mates, on Top of the Pops with a Sensational new song Back Home.

The song composed by Mr Phile Colter and Mr Martin was a hit from the start, winning for the players a Silver Disc. Gordon Banks was the first to receive the Disc as you may have read a little way back in the book.

I bought both the seven-inch 45rpm single and the 33rpm LP, both in vinyl and both of which blared loudly from our 1960s Decca gramophone. *Back Home* still plays in my head and I still smile at the memory of the late Alan Ball's squeaky voice as he and the other players voiced over the last song on the LP, *There'll always be an England.*

Two years later, as the political atmosphere began to sour, these songs would not have been heard in the Creggan; but in the summer of 1970, my hero was Banksy and I wanted England to retain the World Cup.

I lived for each match of the tournament and, as the hours ticked away before kick-off, my nerves would be raw. More than anything, I wanted Gordon Banks to play well. And I wasn't disappointed.

The game against Brazil on Sunday 7 June was billed as the clash of the World Champions. It was played under the merciless heat of a midday sun. The temperature rose to over 100°F. The timing was cruel and reflected the changing values of the game – commercial considerations were beginning to take precedence over the very soul of the sport: its players and the fee-paying public.

Apart from a handful of English supporters, the entire stadium was solidly pro-Brazil. From the outset, England matched the mighty Brazilians, who opted to play a defensive game in the first half, managing only to win a few corners. In fact, apart from some off-target shots, the only Brazilian effort on target became the stuff of legends.

England had been pressing forward and probing. Felix, the Brazilian goalkeeper, was suspect in the air and was found wanting with a Bobby Charlton cross. He was called into action on four occasions in the opening ten minutes.

The magic of football is how the game can ebb and flow, then suddenly explode into life. This contest never ebbed but at times, due to the oppressive heat, it was played at walking pace.

The game is primarily remembered for the culmination of an extraordinary sequence of end-to-end football around the tenth minute when Lee drove a shot towards the Brazilian goal, which Felix had little difficulty in holding. He then rolled the ball into the path of his captain, Carlos Alberto. Seeing Jairzinho make a run, he struck a perfect pass long and hard down the right wing. England's Terry Cooper moved to cover, but with one delicate touch the Brazilian striker left him a floundering spectator. The move drew Bobby Moore and Brian Labone, both making late runs towards Jairzinho.

Gordon Banks, aware that unmarked Tostão was moving

into a scoring position on the near post, moved to cover as Jairzinho connected with the ball on the back-line, just inside the England 18-yard box. Banks watched the ball rise over Tostão's head before realizing it was a beautifully measured pass, soon to be met by perfection on the far side of his goal.

Pelé leapt like a puma. In one graceful, flawless movement he took flight from just outside the England six-yard box. His body arched backwards as though being cocked. Then, magnificently, the hunter within pulled the trigger. His upper body hammered forward, his head turning the ball into a downward projectile. It bounced two feet short of the England goal, a vicious and unstoppable bounce carrying it towards the right post. Pelé felt and knew the sound of conquest as the ball left his head. He roared "Goal!"

The entire Jalisco Stadium rose to their feet to celebrate the magic of the maestro; rose in unison, their cheering and applauding celebrating the inevitable. But, then, the cheering turned to one gigantic gasp of disbelief.

Banks had instantaneously turned, sprinted four paces to make a surely hopeless dive backwards a yard out from his goal line. He dived backwards because Pelé's header had already beaten him as it bounced off the baked surface of the Jalisco stadium. It was continuing its journey into the net.

What happened next almost defies explanation as it was, quite literally, a miracle save.

Banks was in full flight, some three feet off the ground. Seeing the bounce of the ball he somehow managed, in one movement, to bend his body, leaving his legs and thighs suspended in the air. With a gravity defying twist, his falling torso turned skywards allowing his right arm and hand reach backwards to lift the rising ball upwards and over the bar.

The Brazilian supporters thundered respectful applause, the brilliance of the save overcoming their disappointment. Pelé clasped his head in incredulity. Bobby Moore, chasing the play, stood momentarily transfixed before joining the applause. Pelé was later to describe the save as the greatest he had ever seen.

I watched it live on our black and white television with my father in the living room of 41 Leenan Gardens. We knew we were witnesses to a moment that would live forever. I rose from the settee, sure it was a goal. At that instant tens of millions in Brazil were probably doing the same. As the ball fell safely behind the England netting I punched the air and roared, "Great Save Gordon!" I swelled with pride for my hero. The commentator exclaimed, "What a fantastic save by Gordon Banks!" My father simply shook his head and asked, "How did he do that?"

England dominated the rest of the first half but half-time was a welcome relief. Throughout the game, the pitiless sun was unrelenting. The players, instead of chasing their shadows, were running on top of them.

Just before the start of the second half, some lines from Noel Coward's 1932 song, *Mad Dogs and Englishmen*, took on a new kind of theatrical significance as the England team walked back onto the pitch, only to realise they had been lured into a piece of Brazilian gamesmanship:

It seems such a shame when the English claim the earth,

They give rise to such hilarity and mirth.
Ha ha ha ha hoo hoo hoo hoo hee hee hee hee...
Mad dogs and Englishmen go out in the midday sun.

As England took up their positions for the resumption, the Brazilian side of the field was empty. England waited. And waited. For at least five minutes, Brazil did not appear. The only English player who found some cover from the scorching sun was Gordon Banks who, by leaning against his right goalpost, managed to find cover in the narrow shadow cast by the bar. Brazil was happy to let England dehydrate and bake.

In early June 2010, I had the honour of welcoming the great Brazilian captain, Carlos Alberto, to Dublin. During a quiet moment I asked him about the Brazilian delay in resuming the second half. "Was it a deliberate tactic?" I detected the suppression of a smile, but got no response, as though he didn't understand my question. But since our conversation had been about the Brazil vs. England 1970 game and he had expressed the opinion that it was one of the most exemplary football games ever played, I have no doubt the great captain knew exactly what I was asking.

Eventually the game resumed and the quality of football was simply superb. Both teams were evenly balanced with their complements of world-class players. It was end-to-end excitement, with Brazil keeping Banks busy.

Banks' handling throughout was faultless. Inside the first five minutes, he was called into action three times, the third a low spinning diagonal shot from Paolo Cesar that he parried with his fists for a corner.

Brazil began to release men from defence and their midfield started to show greater promise. The English defence – Moore in particular – were solid. His tackling, timing and inspirational presence made him, in my opinion, the man of the match.

As the game progressed, one sensed that the Brazilians were sharpening their blades. Ten minutes into the second half, Pelé sent through a ball that had Banks and Jairzinho on a collision course. Banks reached the ball just outside his penalty area and had kicked it to safety as the Brazilian striker grazed him with a raised boot. The England goal-keeper was furious and protested to the referee, Abraham Klein of Israel, demonstrating Jairzinho's action.

Quarter of an hour in, Rivelino made a run from midfield and at the edge of England's penalty area hit a vicious left footed drive. Banks' positioning was perfect but he only had time to instinctively raise both fists from which the ball thundered some 30-yards up field.

Brazil's pressure was unrelenting as one sensed the inevitable. A minute later they were again on the prowl. From their midfield, Paulo Cesar, Rivelino, Carlos Alberto and Tostão moved the ball swiftly to the right edge of the England 18-yard box. Tostão gathered a rebound off Labone and then combined with Paulo Cesar before attempting to thread the ball through the legs of Moore. In a follow-up tackle Tostão forced the ball past the England captain.

As though connected by radar, the next three moves were sheer magic. Tostão killed the ball, made a 90-degree turn and immediately switched the direction of the game with a delicately delivered chip to the feet of Pelé, who was standing on the England penalty spot. Anticipating a shot, Banks moved to close the angle when suddenly Pelé tapped the ball to his right. It rolled into the path of Jairzinho who hit an unstoppable drive past the diving Banks. The stadium erupted, as the great keeper rolled himself momentarily onto his knees. Brazil had, at last, scored.

When Mr. Klein blew the final whistle it seemed a grave injustice that England had lost, for both teams had justified their reputations, playing a classic of the beautiful game.

At the final whistle, Pelé and Bobby Moore immediately turned to one another. It was Pelé who peeled off his famous number 10 shirt to exchange it with the England captain. Before they parted, Pelé said to Moore, "I'll see you in the Final."

Four decades later, the moment people remember is Gordon Banks' save from Pelé. It survives in the memory of all who had watched the clash of the World Champions and has become one of the great highlights of World Cup history: reverentially recalled as 'That Save'. And, as alluded to by Carlos Alberto above, the game itself is considered by many as one of the finest games ever played.

Having defeated Romania and Czechoslovakia, England advanced to the Quarter-Final on Sunday 14 June, 1970.

On the day of an England match, I was always nervous. As on the previous Sunday, it was family tradition to attend mass at St. Mary's Chapel. A victory for England was prayed for privately, and especially that Gordon Banks would have a good game. In the late afternoon, however, news began to break that Banks was doubtful for the Quarter-Final.

When I saw Chelsea's Peter Bonetti emerge from the

tunnel with the England team my heart sank. An England game without Banks was, for me, like watching Robin without Batman.

On the Friday before the game, Sir Alf had allowed the team the luxury of a beer. Twenty minutes after drinking his, Banks began to feel unwell, the only member of the squad to do so. At first it was thought he had contracted a 24-hour stomach bug similar to what Chelsea's Peter Osgood had already recovered from. But for Banks, the sickness was prolonged.

His illness was such that he didn't even have the energy to travel to the Guanajuato Stadium to watch the match. He stayed in his bed and planned to watch the game on television, broadcast with a 50-minute delay, presumably to encourage locals to see the game live at the stadium.

As the nightmare second half unfolded, Banks, due to the transmission delay, was watching the dream developments of the first half. On the half-hour, Keith Newton found Alan Mullery, who scored his first goal for England. Banks became euphoric four minutes into the second half when a flowing move by England saw Ball, Hurst, Newton and Peters combine to give England a commanding 2-0 lead.

With just 12 minutes remaining, however, it all began to fall apart as Beckenbauer scored and then, in the dying minutes, Seeler levelled with a back header that arched over Bonetti, It was extra time, the 1966 World Cup Final all over again.

In the second half of extra-time the champions were finally dethroned with a Muller winner. For the Germans, it was sweet revenge.

Banks, however, was still living the illusion of England's

lead when the squad returned to the hotel in a dejected state. At first he thought they were playing a practical joke on him but, when he saw the tears of disappointment being shed by Bobby Charlton, he realised it was for real. England was out and he and the England squad would be returning home.

Many have been critical of Peter Bonetti's performance that day. There is even an 'Alternative History' website that asks the question: 'What if Gordon Banks had played?'

Three days after England's defeat, the Labour Party lost the General Election in Britain. The website states that there have been 'various explanations for Labour's defeat':

Wilson blamed the BBC, others blamed the unexpectedly low balance of trade figures, others the knock-on effect of England's defeat – in the words of one cabinet minster "the bug in Gordon Banks' tummy".

Banks, however, knowing the loneliness of a goalkeeper's lot, has remained loyal to Bonetti, recognising how difficult it was for the Chelsea keeper to replace him in such a crucial game at such short notice. All other positions have a covering line behind them, but a goalkeeper only has the canopy of his goal netting. Strikers love to run into it. For a goalkeeper – as he turns, humiliated, and stoops to retrieve a muted ball – that confined and draped area resembles a lonely prison cell.

In the wake of the Quarter-Final, it was reported that Alf Ramsey lamented the loss of Banks: "The one player I could not do without against West Germany was Gordon Banks." After the game *Daily Mirror* sports correspondent Ken Jones found Sir Alf in his hotel room, uncharacteristically nursing a stiff drink.

"It had to be him," Alf said to Jones. "Of all the players to lose, Ken, it had to be him!"

It remains a mystery that only Banks became so ill despite the fact he was consuming the same carefully monitored food and drink as the rest of the squad. Was that Friday night beer spiked?

As a boy, I certainly believed Banks had been poisoned. As an adult, I'm less certain but in truth I would not be surprised if he had been.

I was intrigued by an article I read in the June 8, 2006 edition of the US soccer magazine, *USSoccerPlayers.com*, on the eve of the Germany World Cup, which discussed Banks' sudden illness. The article, penned by Ken Pendleton and entitled *Beautiful Hysteria*, claimed that: 'Brian Granville... probably the most esteemed soccer writer in the English-speaking world...' had given credibility to a story claiming, 'In 1970, the CIA allegedly sabotaged England's chances of winning by poisoning goalkeeper's Gordon Banks' food before the quarterfinal match against West Germany.'

Pendleton continued: 'I'm not kidding... Conspiracy theory has it that our government wanted Brazil to win the World Cup very badly because they thought it would stabilize the government (read: dictatorship) and came to the conclusion that only England, led by its excellent goal-keeper, stood in the way. The story has never been proven, but Banks was the only player to get sick and England went on to lose the quarterfinal, in large part because the man who deputized for Banks, Peter Bonetti, let in a soft goal.

Pendleton went on to express skepticism about the story, stating:

'I don't doubt that the CIA would stoop so low; after all, this is the same underhand bunch that tried to put explosives in Fidel Castro's cigar and poison his shaving cream. But how did they know that they didn't have to worry about Uruguay or Italy, whom Brazil beat in the semifinal and final? Can you picture a bunch of policy wonks sitting around a table, field reports and poisoned pens in hand, debating the merits of Brazil's opponents? 'We got to take out that English goalkeeper. Put our best black bag man in Mexico on the job.'

With tongue-in-cheek, Pendleton humorously continued: 'Let's hope, for the sake of international relations, that the incriminating documents, should they exist, don't get declassified anytime soon. The English public may have stomached the fact that there were no WMDs [Weapons of Mass Destruction] and the implications of the Downing Street memo, but they would probably demand that the Labour Party pull the troops out of Iraq post-haste if it turned out that our government had a hand in scuttling their World Cup chances all those years ago.'

Interestingly, Granville reintroduced this theory during the 2010 South African World Cup, following England's humiliating 4-1 defeat by Germany in Bloemfontein. The controversy that raged around Frank Lampard's disallowed goal inevitably awakened memories of the 1966 World Cup Final and England's defeat by West Germany in the 1970 Mexico Quarter-Final.

In his July 2nd World Cup Diary for *World Soccer* magazine, the legendary British Sports correspondent wrote: 'Though not, I hope, an addict of conspiracy theory... I have steadily come to believe that Banks was the victim of sabotage. This is because Gordon himself assured me a few years ago at an event in Mayfair that far from having drunk "the fatal glass of beer", as I'd quite wrongly believed, he had in fact eaten and drunk exactly what every other member of the squad had done.'

Granville mentions a story told by Bob Oxby, a journalist with the *Telegraph*, whose cousin, Senator Stuart Symington, served the State of Missouri 1953 – 1976. According to Granville, the prominent Republican Senator told Oxby concerning Banks' mysterious illness: "That was the CIA! You don't think we were going to let England beat Brazil, do you?"

Granville alludes to the political motivation: "Brazil at the time being in political turmoil with the prospect of the country turning left."

Whether or not there is truth in this theory, we will probably never know. But it's an interesting perspective and one that only adds to the stature of Banks.

And the 1970 Brazil team certainly didn't need the CIA to help them win the World Cup. Few would argue with the fact they were the greatest and most complete team to ever grace the tournament. One only has to view their fourth goal in the World Cup Final against Italy, scored by captain Carlos Alberto Torres, to see their power, grace and majesty in the kingdom they ruled.

After the Quarter Final I went out into the early evening sunshine to shake off my depression with a game of football on the nearby green. I faced a few taunts from neighbourhood teenagers, but very few. After all, most of us supported English First Division teams and the England squad contained many of our heroes. With England eliminated so too was the intensity of our interest since Northern Ireland, the Republic of Ireland, Scotland and Wales had all failed to qualify for the tournament.

5

A Message in Lipstick

Five days after England's defeat by West Germany, I arrived
home from school to find a message scrawled in lipstick on
the large mirror we had above our mantelpiece. It was
Friday, 19th June, 1970, and my heart raced as I read the
red letters written by my sister Deirdre: 'Don see Journal,
Gordon Banks coming to Donegal'. She had left the *Derry
Journal* on the table with the back page facing up. The two
most important words in my life at that time 'Gordon
Banks' were written in large block capitals on the back page
of our local paper: 'GORDON BANKS WILL PLAY AT
BALLYBOFEY'.

I had only seen Banks on television, in books, magazines
and newspapers. The possibility of seeing him in reality
was unbelievable. I read and re-read the opening words of
the article:

'GORDON BANKS, O.B.E., the Stoke City and
England goalkeeper, will be playing in Finn Park,
Ballybofey, on Sunday, August 2.'

Stoke City were to play local Donegal team, Finn Harps, as

part of a pre-season tour. Harps' manager, Patsy McGowen, said, "Banks, after his displays in the World Cup should draw, on his own, the biggest crowd yet to Finn Park."

And my father, unknown to me, began to plan magic.

However, four days after the *Derry Journal* announcement came news of an immense local tragedy that cast a deep depression over our estate. At breakfast my mother told me of a terrible fire two streets from our own, in Dunree Gardens. A number of people had died, including children. After school, I walked past the terraced house where the tragedy had occurred. Leenan Gardens had been built with red bricks, but Dunree Garden houses were built with concrete, the outside of which was painted with white-wash. The blackened interior was in stark contrast and the scorching above the windows indicated a fierce inferno.

Military Police had arrived on the scene and two officers made desperate efforts to enter the house to try to rescue those trapped. Two adults and a child were dead on arrival at Altnegalvin Hospital and a second child died a few hours later. The children had been in their beds. A third man found in a nearby garden with horrific burns died eleven days later.

It emerged that the three adults were members of the fledgling scantily-equipped and poorly-organised Provisional IRA. They had been making petrol bombs. By comparison with Belfast, Derry was relatively quiet, so this news was greeted with some trepidation by the local population; it indicated the beginning of a new departure for Derry.

A turning point in the initial rapport between the Catholic community and the British Army came on 3 July, 1970.

Following nights of rioting and gunfire, the Army imposed a curfew on the Lower Falls area of Belfast, during which they shot dead three civilians and another was killed when struck by a military vehicle.

Hundreds of houses were raided in search of weapons and ammunition. Residents complained bitterly that the army had been abusive and had caused unnecessary damage to their homes. Thereafter, the army was no longer seen as impartial.

It was hard to believe that only two months had passed since my school's 10-day Adventure Training Course with the British Army. How rapidly things were falling apart. I had just turned 14, Belfast was a world away, and while the Dunree Gardens fire heralded the beginning of war in my hometown, I was incapable of reading the signs at the time. Football was my one and only passion and the Stoke visit couldn't come soon enough, due to the promise of seeing my hero.

The day Stoke City played Finn Harps happened to also be the day the British Army in Belfast fired the first rubber bullet in the conflict: 2nd August, 1970. This was an important development politically, but from a personal perspective, within a couple of years, 10-year-old Richard Moore was hit at point blank range by one such bullet and blinded for life. Richard is five years younger than me and lived in the next street. Our friendship began twenty years ago when I had cause to contact him and, when I mentioned my name, I must admit I was chuffed when he said, "You were the goalkeeper. I remember taking shots against you."

Richard remains unembittered, and has an upbeat personality. Blind he may be, but he has vision of another kind that makes him a great sounding board, wise and insightful.

Memory Making

My father wasn't much into football, but I didn't have to ask him to take me to see the friendly match between Finn Harps and Stoke City. He knew how important Gordon Banks was to his 14-year-old youngest son.

It seemed like an eternity between the lipstick message and 2 August, 1970. The game was played in neighbouring Donegal. What my father did for me that day was an amazing act of understanding and generosity.

Unknown to me, he had hidden my scrapbook in the trunk of our 1964 Vauxhall Victor, a car which he always kept immaculate. We travelled to the game with my mother and a near neighbour, Tony Doherty, of Westway Gardens.

My father had an inkling that the Stoke team would be staying at Jackson's Hotel, Ballybofey, hometown of Finn Harps FC. He pulled into the hotel's car park and told me to wait. I paid no attention as he went to the trunk and somehow managed to conceal from me that he was carrying my scrapbook into the hotel.

A few minutes later he emerged, elated and excited, beckoning vigorously. Puzzled, I followed him into the hotel lobby and immediately spotted my prized scrapbook on the desk with a tall man leafing through it. "Here he is, Mr. Banks," my father said. And, with that, Gordon Banks turned around.

Words cannot describe the meaning of that moment. To me, it was like being granted an audience with God.

He smiled, warmly, shook my hand and immediately we began to talk goalkeeping. His sensitivity and respect towards my parents and this Irish kid are a cherished memory. I still remember the lesson received that day from the maestro of the art: "Play lots of table tennis for your reflexes, basketball for your handling and always aim to take a high cross at your highest point."

We discussed the save against Pelé but, with characteristic modesty, he downplayed it and talked instead about the less spectacular block he made against Rivelino who, in the high altitude of Guadalajara Stadium, had thundered a shot towards the England goal. Mr. Banks told me that he considered that to be, perhaps, the best save he made that day, but that it was seldom referred to. He said the shot left Rivelino's boot like a bullet to which he instinctively put up his fists.

It is no exaggeration to say that my life changed that day. After meeting Banksy, my confidence went sky-high and my goalkeeping continued to improve. My biggest regret is that we didn't own a camera and the moment went unrecorded. I do, however, have the autograph that Mr Banks signed at the front of the scrapbook. And, of course, I have the subsequent events that complete this story.

But, most importantly, I have my favourite memory of my father and what he did for me.

6

Banks Blows His Top – Stoke City 1970-72

The Stoke team of the early 70s always performed respectably in the English First Division League and I followed their performances avidly. However, when it came to knockout competitions, the team seemed to revel in living on the edge. It was in the FA Cup and League Cup that Stoke City reached the top and, eventually, won the first major trophy in the club's long history.

In the 1970/71 and 1971/72 seasons, Stoke City twice reached the Semi-Final of the FA Cup. On both occasions they lost to Arsenal after replays. They had no reason to fear mighty Arsenal who would do the League and Cup double in 1971. Earlier in the season, they had not only demolished the Gunners at their Victoria Ground in a 5-0 humiliation, but a 25 yard rocket from Terry Conroy, at the end of a six-man build-up, was voted 'Goal of the Month' and runner-up in 'Goal of the Season' on the BBC's *Match of the Day*.

The first Semi-Final was played in Banks' home city, at

Sheffield Wednesday's ground, Hillsborough. Stoke's captain, Peter Dobing, was injured so Banks was given the honour of captaining the team for the Semi-Final.

From the start, Stoke took the play to Arsenal and were 2-0 up by half time with goals from Denis Smith and John Ritchie. However, shortly after the restart, the Gunners scored and, as Banks admits, "the jitters set in". Stoke rebuffed the Gunners bombardment and deep into injury time, were literally only seconds away from an historic Cup Final appearance.

Then, suddenly, controversy reigned. Banks jumped to collect a George Armstrong cross but found himself on the end of an aerial tackle from which he spilled the ball over the back line. He was certain referee Pat Partridge would award a free kick for a foul against him, but to his amazement Partridge awarded a corner to Arsenal. The Gunners captain, Frank McLintock met the incoming corner with his head and sent it goal-wards. All Banks could do was watch as his Welsh team-mate, John Mahoney, dived full-length and tipped the ball wide. Partridge pointed to the penalty spot. The Gunners scored and escaped the gallows.

The headlines of the press cutting in my scrapbook capture the drama: 'Last-gasp Penalty Row – BANKS BLOWS HIS TOP,' wrote the *Sports Mirror* Reporter. Another headline: 'Even for Banks, it can all turn bitter.' A photograph shows him shaking hands with Arsenal keeper Bob Wilson after the game. He is dejected. The text alongside the picture reads:

'Football has been good to Gordon Banks. But even for its most favoured sons, even for the best goalkeeper in the world, the game can go sour. So it was with the usually so gay Gordon, who was within a minute of Wembley and the F.A. Cup final... Banks, a bitter Banks, insisted that Arsenal should have never been given the corner... "I had the ball knocked out of my hand. It should have been a free-kick to us, not a penalty to them." And most of the 55,000 who packed Hillsborough for a record £80,000 take, were on Banks' side... wherever the Cup finishes up this season, the Stoke-Arsenal semi-final will always be remembered as one of those highly emotional occasions when football snubbed one of its favourite sons.'

On page 429 of my scrapbook, I wrote on April Fool's Day, 1971, the day after the replay: 'Gordon Banks. Oh God. Stoke have been knocked out of the FA Cup semi-final by Arsenal who beat them 2-0 after their lucky 2-2 draw last Saturday.'

After 107 years of waiting, the Stoke City cabinet was still bereft of a major trophy.

An Irishman with a dilemma

I saw Gordon Banks play one more time, when England came to Windsor Park, Belfast, for a home international in May, 1971. It was the controversial game when a mischievous George Best, who had clearly studied the England goalkeeper's unique kick outs, suddenly pounced. He interrupted the pull of gravity with his foot as Banksy tossed the ball up, and left the keeper floundering as he headed the ball into the back of the England net.

Windsor Park went wild. But I was an Irishman with a dilemma. As a goalkeeper, I believed it to be a foul. But, even if it had been legitimate, how could I celebrate a goal being scored against my hero? When the referee disallowed the goal, I had to contain myself.

I later learned that I wasn't the only Irishman with a dilemma. There was another one, playing that day opposite Banksy – the legendary Irish goalkeeper, Pat Jennings. In an interview for this book, I asked him if he thought George Best's goal should have been allowed.

He responded: "No, because the very next week at Old Trafford George did exactly the same thing against me. Only at Manchester the goal stood because of the controversy from the week before, between him and Banksy. I played in both games, literally from one week to the next. Because the referee disallowed the first one, when George put his foot up across me I stopped because I was going to break my leg or break his. You can't have people coming in and putting a foot up, or across you, when you are going to kick the ball out. However, despite the controversy from the week before, the referee allowed George's goal against me.

"Gordon did throw the ball a fair bit away from his body every time he went to kick it out. He had a different technique from the rest of us. But, you can imagine it would be a disaster, a nightmare, if people were allowed to stick up a foot or put a leg across a goalkeeper every time you wanted to kick the ball out."

7

My best friend

St. Joseph's Secondary School had two enthusiastic managers of the under-13 and under-15 teams, Mr. Paul Duffy and Mr. John Dunne. Mr. Duffy was our music teacher and choirmaster, and helped us win silverware for the school cabinet every year at various singing competitions. One of the great incentives he offered for choir practice was an hour of indoor football in the school gym. It was he who recommended me to the manager of the schools most senior team, John Dunne – a gentle giant.

My friendship with my best friend Shaunie McLaughlin began on the old grass pitch of St. Joseph's School, when we played against his team, Derry Athletic Football Club. During our second and closely fought encounter, Shaunie ran into my penalty area and met a cross from my left with a superbly timed volley. I took flight and not only stopped it, I caught the ball on my chest in mid-air. One of his team-mates, a big centre forward named Frankie Doherty, ran in hoping I would spill it upon landing. When he saw I had a firm grip, he exclaimed: "Great Save keeper!"

For a moment Shaunie's eyes and mine met. I still think

of that save as the best of my life. More importantly, it was to be the beginning of my first real friendship.

Interestingly, St. Joseph's centre forward that day was Hillary Carlyle, a tall fair-haired pupil from Creggan Broadway. Hillary later went on to play in the North American Soccer League (NASL) for the Las Vegas Quicksilvers and even played against Gordon Banks. I recall, some years later, a news photograph in the local paper showed him breaking-up an altercation between two of football's greatest icons, Pelé, then playing for the New York Cosmos, and Eusebio, a team-mate of Hillary's. I was filled with pride that a former team-mate was playing alongside players who were heroes of our boyhood dreams.

After that game, I was invited by Jim O'Hea to join Derry Athletic FC. It wasn't long before Shaunie and I were spending hours together almost everyday practising: Shaunie shooting, me saving. Not surprisingly, his hero was Pelé. Shaunie had recently returned from a spell with Leicester City's youth team and was soon off to Edinburgh to play for Hibernians. We became best friends, and in time soulmates.

We could see that the Irish 'Troubles' were not happening in a vacuum. No side in the conflict, official or paramilitary, can pretend that it has not been responsible for dreadful deeds. There was no high moral ground. And, while we dreamed of becoming professional footballers, we could not escape from the political tempest that raged around us.

Shaunie and I trained at Oakland Park, enclosed on all sides by terraced houses, even as gun battles raged around the Creggan. One evening, in the small changing hut where we kitted out, I was boasting of throwing stones at the

British Army. Suddenly, I felt the full force of a boot on my backside. When I turned around I had the livid face of our manager, Jim O'Hea, bearing down on me. He told me on no uncertain terms that if I was to engage in that kind of activity I wasn't welcome in the club.

I felt humiliated, but I didn't dare speak back to the manager. He had his idiosyncrasies, like Alf Ramsey, but he cared for his boys and he ran his club like an extended family. He tried desperately to keep our minds focused on football and well away from politics. He was a good man, and I knew that even then. So his boot on my arse, sore and humiliating though it was, wasn't enough to break the bond. He sent me home that night, quiet, and deep in thought.

Plunged into Crisis: The End of Innocence

The 'Troubles' intensified and things went from bad to worse. On 8 July, 1971, the Army shot dead Seamus Cusack and Desmond Beattie in Derry. Then followed the introduction of Internment without Trial on 9 August, 1971 and Bloody Sunday, 30 January, 1972. I participated in the Civil Rights march that day, my first ever, and was standing only two feet away from 17-year-old Michael Kelly (neighbouring Dunmore Gardens goalkeeper), when he was fatally shot. I can still hear him gasp as a ricochet bullet punctured his flesh.

An instant later, confusion and terror reigned; the rubble barricade began to spit dust as bullets thundered into it. I am unable to recall accurately the events of those horrific moments of my adolescence. I am still conscious of people to my right crying out and falling close to me at the barricade. Then, suddenly, the wall of an apartment above my head burst, showering those below with brick and mortar.

A primeval instinct took possession of me, and, unashamedly, I started running home to safety. "Son, what's happening?" a woman's voice called as I passed her. "There must be at least six people dead," I shouted back. Her face registered disbelief but I didn't stop to convince her.

The following day my best friend, Shaunie McLaughlin, called for me and we retraced our steps. I remember pointing to the bullet mark on the wall above where I had been the previous afternoon. We looked with incredulity at the bloodstains on the pavements and by the barricade. Across the road, in a first-story apartment, one window had six bullet holes with cracks spreading out like webs. The blue and white civil rights banner that led our procession the previous day was now heavily stained with the blood of Barney McGuigan, a father of six children who was shot while holding aloft a white handkerchief as he had cautiously made his way to the aid of a fatally wounded man. He was killed by a shot to the back of the head.

On the day of the funerals, Shaunie and I stood silently together in the cold rain that wept over Derry as cortège after cortège slowly made their way towards the cemetery gates.

We were numb, confused and increasingly angry.

Over thirty years later, I would sit in the public gallery at Central Hall, Westminster, as Soldier F of the Parachute Regiment in 1972 admitted under cross-examination that in addition to three other people he had also killed Mr.

McGuigan.

Ironically, the courtroom drama I witnessed was in the very same hall from where the Jules Rimet Trophy was stolen in 1966, prior to the start of that year's World Cup Finals.

Bloody Sunday was a bitter experience, especially after the whitewash of the Widgery Tribunal. Memories of that tragic day still give rise to anger and outrage within me. The atmosphere began to change dramatically as a direct consequence. Boys I played football with were making other choices. The IRA thereafter had many willing recruits and I seriously considered making that choice too.

A Ghostly Gordon Banks

Despite the 'Troubles', there were also moments of relief. I began using an old 8mm projector owned by my father. Occasionally, I'd show silent Charlie Chaplin and Laurel and Hardy movies to neighbourhood children.

In the early '70s, to help fundraise for Derry Athletic FC, I built up a regular ticket round on Friday evenings. A friend, Paddy McLaughlin, came with me and our last call at around 9.30pm was not to sell tickets but to meet up with our babysitting girlfriends. An unexpected additional reward for the ticket round came in 1971 when, as the club's main fundraiser, I got an award of a three-minute 8mm black and white film of Gordon Banks in action in the 1966 World Cup Finals.

In this era of YouTube and DVDs, instant access to our heroes in action is the press of a button or a mouse click away. Back then, however, the idea of owning my own three-minute movie on Banksy was a source of great excitement. I was also very moved by Jim's thoughtfulness in securing it as a reward for all my fundraising for the club.

One night I set up the projector at the back bedroom window, aimed at the whitewashed wall of Gallagher's house some twenty yards away. The image was visible as milky shadows moving on the wall, and so big it spilled over to a second house. Here was a ghostly Gordon Banks making spectacular dives across the back walls and bedroom windows of Melmore Gardens.

I was thrilled. But it created great commotion among neighbourhood children who had spotted the eerie figures dancing on the walls. They were certain it was an apparition. I went out to explain and had to re-run the film, initially to reassure them and then to endlessly entertain them.

8

Banks' Favourite Save & Wembley Swansong

As the Spring of 1972 began, Stoke City regained their battling cup form. Once again they reached the FA Cup Semi-Final, and once again their opponents were Arsenal. Again it went to a replay and, unbelievably, again controversy reigned due to a refereeing decision.

Twenty minutes into the game, having weathered considerable Arsenal pressure, Stoke's Jimmy Greenhoff was upended by Frank McLintock inside the penalty area. The referee pointed to the penalty spot and Greenhoff put Stoke ahead. Ten minutes into the second half Arsenal winger George Armstrong jostled with Stoke captain Peter Dobing inside the Stoke penalty area. Referee Keith Walker pointed to the penalty spot for the second time. Charlie George beat Banks and the sides were level.

Ten minutes later, Stoke City's hopes were truly dashed when Radford scored, but from an offside position. It was the last straw for many of the Stoke players. Referee Walker had been chasing the ball from the Gunners' half.

The Stoke players protested that he should consult his lineman, Bob Matthewson. He duly did, while the Stoke and Arsenal fans held their breaths.

Banks was confident that Matthewson would set the record straight. To everyone's amazement, Walker turned from his lineman and headed for the centre circle. The goal was allowed!

Banks said the dressing room afterwards resembled a morgue. Jackie Marsh summed up all the players feelings when he said, "I'd rather be beaten 4-0 and know we had lost fair and square than to go out like that." Later, when Marsh was asked what, in his opinion, was the turning point of the game, he replied, "When the linesman turned up."

Stoke City's disappointment, however, was tempered by their equally epic and historic campaign that had culminated the month previously in the club's first ever Wembley final, in the League Cup. But it was that campaign that convinced them they had the beating of the best and made their defeat by Arsenal so disillusioning.

The fourth round had seen the beginning of their epic climb to the summit of Wembley Stadium. Drawn against league leaders, Manchester United, it took three games to decide the tie. Captain Peter Dobing and John Ritchie cancelled out a magnificent George Best goal in the second replay to allow Stoke to advance to a fifth round clash with Bristol Rovers. They beat Rovers 4-2 and faced West Ham United in the Semi-Final, played over two matches.

Stoke lost their home game 2-1, a Geoff Hurst penalty and Clyde Best goal demolishing the lead Peter Dobing had given them. The second leg at Upton Park was not only epic – in extra time it produced Gordon Banks' favourite save.

With three minutes of extra time remaining and looking set for a replay, West Ham assaulted the Stoke goalmouth. Desperation and confusion led to an incident involving Harry Redknapp and Gordon Banks, which the referee adjudged was a penalty. Memories of the previous season's Semi-Final against Arsenal caused the hopes of Stoke City's supporters to sink deeper than the Titanic.

Geoff Hurst, who had already beaten Banks with his penalty in the first leg at Stoke, stepped up. The silence of the faithful at Upton Park was striking. As Hurst made a long run towards the ball, Banks gambled that he would repeat his first leg penalty and so dived to his right. The drive was powerful but Banks was equal to it and sent the ball over the bar and into the night air.

The Stoke players, almost resigned to yet another Semi-Final defeat, couldn't believe their eyes. Banks was besieged with congratulations from team-mates as they arrived in the penalty box. For the Stoke fans, Banks' save against England's World Cup hat-trick hero was even sweeter than his 1970 save against Pelé in Guadalajara. He had given his club the kiss of life.

The replay, at Hillsborough, ended in a scoreless draw after extra time. The second replay, at Old Trafford, was finally settled when Dublin-born Terry Conroy, known at Stoke as the 'Wizard of the Wing', scored Stoke's third goal in a 3-2 classic.

At last, Stoke were bound for Wembley. Their opponents, Chelsea, were hot favourites on Saturday 4th March, 1972.

I turned sixteen the day before the League Cup Final and spent my birthday in a state of nervous excitement. Unlike the FA Cup Final, the League Cup wasn't televised live, so I tuned into the radio. In this age of corporate football, in which matches arc screened almost daily, the magic of live radio broadcasting might seem a poor option. In the early 70s it was the only option.

I sat alone in the sitting room of my home at Leenan Gardens, but my mind was in Wembley with the almost 98,000 fans. My imagination was set ablaze by the BBC Radio Two commentator, Simon Smith. This was a classic match, as was confirmed by the highlights shown the following day on *The Big Match*. But the excitement of a live radio commentary, as one pulsates and perspires with every kick of the ball, is spellbinding. Imagination fills the gaps as the pictures run through the mind, painted by the commentator. Smith was magical, the excitement in his voice firing on all cylinders. Throughout the game, I was on the edge of my seat, constantly jumping to my feet or dropping to my knees as thc ecstasy and the agony of the Wembley Cup Final filled the room.

Terry Conroy, once again, produced his wizardry, this time along the Wembley wings. Terry was a firebrand whose long, flowing red hair sometimes resembled a burning firecracker as he took off on the wing. Despite his distinctive hair colour, however, he was not renowned for scoring with his head. But that was to change and his most revered goal among Stoke fans to this day is Stoke City's opener in the League Cup Final.

Just four minutes into the game, a Jimmy Greenhoff shot deflected off Chelsea's David Webb and rose perfectly for a header, which TC arched beyond the reach of Peter

Bonetti in the Chelsea goal. It was the dream start. Banksy and Conroy would have heard my roar of delight but for the cascades of jubilation on the terraces from fans who had travelled from the Midlands to witness history in the making.

I was much more subdued at half-time, however, as I made myself a cup of tea on our gas cooker. Chelsea's big Peter Osgood had managed to recover from a tumble and, while still on the floor, somehow swivelled his lanky right leg and yanked the ball past Banks for an equaliser.

The tension and drama of the second-half filled every sentence uttered by Smith. In the 73rd minute, I could sense a significant Stoke build-up in the pitch of his voice. Conroy raced past Chelsea's Ron Harris on the right and floated an inch perfect cross to 'Big John' Ritchie, Stoke's leading goalscorer, at the far-post.

Ritchie had noticed fellow striker Jimmy Greenhoff bearing down on the Chelsea goal and with the gentlest of touches laid the ball at his feet. Greenhoff's volley brought out a magnificent parrying save from Peter Bonnetti. Thirty-five year-old Eastham, the oldest man on the pitch, roared at Smith to get out of the way as he pounced on the rebound and struck gold for Stoke.

I raced from the sitting room and, taking the stairs three at a time, burst into my bedroom. I jumped on my bed and placed two smackers on my Stoke City team poster over the heads of Conroy and Eastham, both sitting together in the photo on the right of the front.

The last 15-minutes were filled with nerve-racking excitement as the mighty Chelsea upped a gear. Could Stoke hold out and break their apparent jinx?

Save of the Century. Banks claws Pelé's header over the bar in the 1970 World Cup clash between World Champions, England and Brazil. *From an Alan Damms painting.*

Finally, 'The Photograph'! Gordon Banks and Don Mullan in conversation during their 2nd meeting, 18 March 2005. *Carl Mullan.*

1970. Derry Athletic Football Club under-18 five-aside team, winners of the *Daily Express* regional finals. Manager Jim O'Hea presents the trophy to captain, Seamus McDowell. Shaunie McLaughlin (15) is second left and Don Mullan (14), second right. *Willie Carson*

1963: In Full Flight. Gordon Banks showing his amazing reflexes and agility as he pulls off a superb save during training with the England squad at Roehampton, just prior to his 3rd full cap against The Rest of the World. *Courtesy of Banks family collection*

Happy Family. Leicester City and England goalkeeper Gordon Banks with his wife Ursula and their first child, Robert. *Courtesy of Banks family collection*

30 July 1966. Gordon Banks and Sir Alf Ramsey embrace at the end of the World Cup Final. Until his accident in October 1972, Banks was Ramsey's undisputed first choice England goalkeeper. *Courtesy of Banks family collection*

Scrapbook: Banks saves from George Best as Alex Elder covers. *Patrick Walshe*

Scrapbook: In action against Arsenal's John Radford. *Patrick Walshe*

Front row:
David Herd
John Mahoney
Roy Vernon
Peter Dobing
Willie Stevenson
Gerry Conroy
George Eastham

Centre row:
Harry Burrows
Mike Bernard
Eric Skeels
Gordon Banks
Alex Elder
John Marsh
Tony Lacey

Back row:
F. Street (trainer)
Tony Allen
John Ritchie
Dennis Smith
Alan Bloor
Frank Mountford (trainer)

Scrapbook: Gordon Banks' bitterest football memory. Robbed in the FA Cup semi-final by Arsenal. *Patrick Walshe*

Reunion. The heroes of the March 1972 League Cup Final gather for a reunion at Stoke City in March 2005. (Left to Right) Back Row: Darren Cole (Sponsor of reunion), Denis Smith, Alan Bloor, Terry Conroy, John Mahoney, Carl Holness (Sponsor); Front Row: Mike Bernard, John Marsh, Gordon Banks, Jimmy Greenhoff and Mike Pejic [Missing: George Eastham, Peter Dobing and John Richie]. *Carl Mullan*

GORDON BANKS WILL PLAY AT BALLYBOFEY

STOKE TO VISIT FINN PARK

GORDON BANKS, O.B.E., the Stoke City and England goalkeeper, will be playing in Finn Park, Ballybofey, on Sunday, August 2.

Finn Harps Manager Patsy Blackwood received a letter yesterday confirming that Stoke will be playing a friendly game in Ballybofey during their short tour of Ireland.

Said Patsy: "Banks, after his displays in the World Cup series, should draw, on his own, the biggest crowd yet to Finn Park. Because of the great number of people we expect to come we're considering to have been a game between two clubs who have become very friendly during the close season and nobody was going to make anything out of it."

The match with Bohemians was arranged two months ago.

Coaching Course

Finn Harps are to set at home at a three-day coaching machine

GREYHOUNDS

TONIGHT'S DERRY CARD

NO — Tippy Tumble, De Patsy, Slingshot, Wonder, Lovely Captain, Bronwing Hann, Parnes, Bonnarris Silver, Sid—Parton Karen, De Cos...

Derry Journal Headlines: 19 June 1970. *Patrick Walshe*

West German goalkeeper, Hans Tilkowski (left) with Gordon Banks' hero, Bert Trautmann (right), at a training session during the 1966 World Cup Finals in England.
Photo: Courtesy of Hans Tilkowski

Another Hero. Don's father, Charles, meets his sporting hero, Champion Scottish rally driver, Jimmy McRae, on the Circuit of Ireland.
Don Mullan

Happy Days. Banks and Best enjoying each other's company. *Courtesy of Banks family collection*

4 March 1972: Joy unbounded. Celebrating Stoke City's historic League Cup victory at Wembley. *Courtesy of Banks family collection*

Peacemaker. Hillary Carlyle, St. Joseph's under-15 centre forward, moves in to break-up an altercation between two of the world's greatest footballers, Brazil's Pelé and Portugal's Eusebio, during his sojourn in the NASL with the Las Vegas Quicksilvers. *Courtesy of Carlyle family collection*

2005. Gordon Banks and the hands that helped England win the World Cup. *Carl Mullan.*

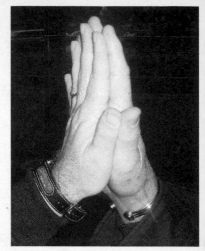

Hands of Friendship. Mullan and Banks. *Carl Mullan*

Holding History. Gordon Banks and Carl Mullan hold the blue aertex shirt Gordon wore when he made 'That Save' from Pelé in the 1970 Mexico World Cup. *Don Mullan*

In his autobiography, Banks does not write about his role in the game, but on several occasions Smith's voice screamed as he applauded the Stoke and England goalkeeper. None more so than in the dying seconds, when Mike Bernard decided to knock the ball all the way back to Banks from just outside the centre circle. George Eastham later joked that it was the best through ball of the game – and for Chelsea it was. The back pass split the Stoke defence and Chelsea's Chris Garland raced to collect his gift. Watching it on TV the next day confirmed for me that this was Banks' best save of the game and epitomised everything that was brilliant about him.

Banks had been standing on his six-yard box when Bernard struck the ball. He immediately picked up on Garland's run and raced to the edge of his box. Neither Garland nor Banks were prepared to hold back. The momentum of both men was such that, immediately after Garland's shot ricocheted off Banks' right knee for a corner, one could almost feel the hard whack of bones. Both men lay injured. Garland was prostrate, having fallen like a warrior taken out by a marksman. Banks was nursing his left ankle.

The game was held up for several minutes before Stoke defended the last corner of the game. There was a touching moment as Chelsea's John Hollins walked over to check on Banks and, with the Stoke trainer, helped him to his feet. As Banks turned to hobble back to his goal line, Hollins patted him on the back. It was a sign of the respect, esteem and affection opponents, as well as team-mates, had for him.

Banks rose to punch the incoming corner but referee Burtenshaw blew for a foul on him. As Banks' free kick headed towards Chelsea's half of Wembley, Burtenshaw blew the final whistle.

Wembley and the streets of Stoke-on-Trent triumphed. While all football enthusiasts felt sorry for Chelsea, across the British and Irish Isles most were happy for Stoke. I went on an Indian war dance of delight. It was the best birthday gift imaginable. Outside, there was turmoil and pain on the streets around us, but football was a cocoon, a place of retreat – somewhere to find escape.

Stoke City Football Club, after 108 years of competitive football, had, at long last, won a major trophy.

There was poignancy about Banks' appearance on that 4th March, 1972. Unknown to him, unknown to us all, as a club player this was his Wembley swansong and his penultimate Wembley appearance. He would play one more Wembley international for England seven weeks later against West Germany. He was living proof that goalkeepers can reach their prime in their 30s, at an age when most outfield players are considered to have reached their sell-by date. The consistency of his performances for Stoke City and England throughout the 1971-72 season was to culminate in him being named Footballer of the Year. Banks was on a roll, but he was soon to learn that life is tenuous and cannot be taken for granted.

A Bank Robbery Back in Derry

As political change and turmoil raged in Derry, I continued to train and play for my school and for Derry Athletic Football Club. The manager, Jim O'Hea, was also a scout for Gordon Banks' previous team, Leicester City. Jim's life was coaching football and it was all done voluntarily. He had a good eye for goalkeepers and two who benefited from his guidance were Packie Bonner (Glasgow Celtic) and Shay Given (Newcastle United) who both went on to play for the Republic of Ireland. He also produced, among others, two Northern Ireland internationals for Leicester City, John O'Neill and Paul Ramsey.

One day around May, 1972 Jim called at my home in a panic. I was 16-years-and-two-months when he told me he had to elevate me immediately to the senior team as its goalkeeper had just been caught, allegedly, in a bank robbery in the nearby seaside town of Buncrana. We were shocked, but it was a sign of the times.

I made my senior debut in the Quarter and Semi-Finals of the Derry and District Cup, which we won. The final was on Sunday, 28 May, 1972, in the famous Brandywell Stadium. I was the youngest player on the pitch that evening and was weighed down by the responsibility, especially since we were the underdogs against Buncrana Hearts, who had already won the League and were hunting for the double. A number of their players had played for semi-professional teams in the League of Ireland and the Irish League. My father had never been to see me play a football game but, shortly into the first half, I was surprised to hear him shout words of encouragement from the terraces to my right.

From kick-off I kept thinking of how Gordon Banks would approach the game: 'Keep a cool head, marshal the defence, be conscious of positioning at all times, take the ball at your highest point, do things simply, be ready to come off the line, show no fear...'

I played the game of my life and, when our substitute, Seamus McDaid, scored the only goal of the game with three minutes to go, I ran the length of the pitch to congratulate him. It was a glorious evening, especially when Jim O'Hea later came to my home with the trophy and said he'd like me to have it for a few months. Hearing my father recount my performance with obvious pride made it a night to remember.

The following Tuesday, the team photograph was published in the *Derry Journal* alongside a write-up that mentioned I had pulled of some fine saves in the first half. At school, our English teacher Brian Rainey, who had played in the Derry and District League for many years, led my class in a round of applause.

Checkpoint

Shortly after the school holidays began in the summer of 1972, I was sent for a month to cousins in Carrickfergus, Co. Antrim. On my return, my father picked me up at the Railway Station and we headed for home. The Creggan and Bogside were, by now, no-go areas openly patrolled by the IRA. While entering the Creggan we were stopped at an IRA checkpoint. As my father's licence was being checked I eyed the various gunmen from the front passenger seat. To my left, hunkering beside a small, dark green electricity box surrounded by hedges was a young man dressed in blue denim jeans, wearing a red t-shirt and holding an old WWI Lee Enfield single shot rifle. The eyes behind the mask were looking at me.

I knew the look. And he knew I recognised him. It was Shaunie, my best friend.

My heart began to pound. I didn't smile and I never said a word to my father as we continued home. Parents were the last to find out about such developments.

I offloaded my suitcase and immediately headed for Shaunie's house. His sister Maria opened the door. "Do you know what I know?" I asked her. She led me upstairs and nervously pulled, from under a bed, a grey ceremonial tunic. My head was spinning for I knew that Shaunie had made a life-changing decision. I waited for his return. We went into his bedroom and closed the door. In whispered tones, he told me he had joined the auxiliary IRA, a part-time wing of the Provisional IRA. He gave Bloody Sunday as a major reason for his decision.

I said to him, "Shaunie, if you're in, I'm in."

That night he brought me to a recruitment officer's home. We knocked at a door but he was out. A short time later, probably within days, Shaunie was told that the IRA had decided to disband the auxiliaries and that members had a choice of leaving or becoming fully fledged members. Shaunie left. The pressure was off.

Shaunie had once told me that he thought the word 'compassion' was the most beautiful in the English language. In my heart, I knew the path of violence would not be his, let alone my own. Football, once again, dominated our thoughts.

9

The Soldier & the Scrapbook

On many nights I lay awake listening to gun battles around the Creggan Estate. Occasionally, large explosions shook the windows of my bedroom while red tracer bullets streaked across the roofs of our terraced houses like burning meteorites. Sometimes, army flares lit up the night and an artificial daylight would envelop my bedroom.

The walls were covered with portraits, action shots and team posters of just one person – Gordon Banks. One at the foot of the bed was framed. Morning and night he smiled at me. He was like a friend who lived in my mind. And he was the first choice goalkeeper of the country from which many of the soldiers whom we were growing to hate came from.

'Operation Motorman' dismantled the no-go areas on the 31 July, 1972. It was a massive military invasion involving thousands of British soldiers and hundreds of vehicles, including Centurion tanks, aimed at re-establishing a military presence in the Bogside and Creggan.

As Shaunie and I walked between our homes in upper and lower Creggan we were constantly stopped by foot patrols and army checkpoints looking for identification. It

was a whole new experience and, as Irish youngsters, we
resented it.

Early one morning the British Army raided our home. I
was awakened by the roar of Land Rover engines, the
slamming of doors and sound of heavy boots running up
our front steps. Fists banging on the front door were
accompanied by English voices warning us that if the door
wasn't opened immediately it would be smashed. I jumped
up in my bedroom at the front of the house and shouted to
my parents that it was an Army raid and to get out of bed.

I was swept aside as a raiding party of eight or ten
soldiers burst into the house. I followed four upstairs,
fearful for my parents and also because rumours abounded
of soldiers planting guns and ammunition to implicate a
household. My mother had managed to pull on her dressing
gown; my father was standing in his pyjamas. I could see
real fear in their eyes. Mum was on the verge of tears. It
was a humiliating experience to watch parents ordered to sit
quietly while their castle was pulled apart.

I followed one soldier into my bedroom. Then it was
hard to see the humour in the moment, but now I look back
and smile at the confused expression on his face. In his
mind's eye he was probably expecting to find Republican
or IRA paraphernalia adorning my walls. His mouth opened
with incredulity at the sight of large posters of the England
and Stoke City football teams and, of course, many action
shots and portraits of Gordon Banks. I told him that the
England goalkeeper was my hero and pulled my scrapbook
from under the bed to show him.

"Sir!" he called, "Look at this!" Perhaps thinking a
weapon had been found, the officer-in-charge came in. I

could hear my mother calling, "Is everything all right Don?" Several of the raiding party, including their officer, were momentarily distracted as they looked through my Gordon Banks scrapbook and pointed out to one another my prized autograph.

After seeing the scrapbook, they tempered their aggression, much to the relief of my parents. I ended up sitting on our stairway talking to the soldiers about Irish history and why as Irish people we increasingly saw them as occupiers.

"Think about it," I said. "If the shoe was on the other foot and we were the more powerful nation and Irish soldiers were doing to you in England what you are doing to us in Ireland, would you like it?"

It was an extraordinary encounter and, when word came through the radio that I was to be arrested, the officer-in-charge, when he saw my mother begin to cry, went to her and assured her that I would not be hurt.

A small group of mothers from neighbouring homes had gathered in the darkness at the bottom of our steps. Two were carrying umbrellas as there was light drizzle. I can still see them clearly: Mrs Millar, Mrs. Morrison, Mrs McCallion, Mrs Fleming and Mrs. Brolly. I can still hear Mrs. McCallion as she saw me emerge from the house with the soldiers. "Ah! They're taking young Don and he's such a good wee fella!"

One of the women shouted words of protest as I was put into the back of a Land Rover and driven away. A young soldier, sitting towards the open rear doors shouted back and I was shocked to hear myself tell him to leave her alone as she was my neighbour. We both looked at the officer, who was smiling at me.

I was brought to Piggery Ridge British Army post, which sat in the countryside just above the Creggan Estate. I was made to stand in a plain windowless room on my own. I don't recall being photographed or questioned, but after about an hour the officer came to me and said I was free to go home. I could sense that he liked me – I have no doubt the Gordon Banks scrapbook and wall posters had caused him to see me in a different light.

He then stunned me with what was a genuine offer. "Would you like a lift home?" All I could do was laugh. "You must be joking," I answered. "I'll walk home myself."

In different political and historical circumstances, these were men I probably could have grown to like. Most of them were from working class backgrounds and in that regard we had a lot in common. However, I could not ignore our post-Bloody Sunday reality and the fact that many of my contemporaries were now sworn enemies of the British Army. Getting dropped off by a British Army Land Rover at my home would have been wide open to misinterpretation and, quite possibly, danger. It would have been akin to an Iraqi youth being dropped off at his home in the razed city of Fallujah by US Marines following the November 2004 battle.

Dawn had broken during the hour I had been at the Army post. I could see chimneys blowing smoke across the neat rows of terraced houses. The green copper roof of St. Mary's Church was the dominant feature on the local landscape. There was relief as I entered my home. The neighbourhood mothers, many of whom knew what my mother was experiencing, were comforting her with a cup of tea before a blazing fire at our sitting room hearth.

Shaunie's Question

One Sunday, at the beginning of the 1972-73 football season, while Shaunie and I watched *The Big Match* in the living room of his home, a British Army foot patrol walked down Circular Road where he lived. The patrol stopped for a breather and one of the soldiers took up a crouching position just outside the window. Shaunie and I fell silent as we looked at the young man behind the uniform. It was a warm sunny afternoon and, as he wiped sweat beads from his brow, we could see fear in his eyes. He was no more than four or five feet away from us with only a wall and a window in between.

Shaunie then asked a life-changing question that affected me deeply. Referring to the young soldier he said: "When you see him as a human being, how could you kill him?"

There were many reasons why I never made the progression to the IRA. That question of Shaunie's was one of them. So too were my mother, father and our football manager, Jim O'Hea. But, without a doubt, my hero-worship of Banks was also an important factor. My respect for a man who had such a positive impact on my life helped contain my rage. I just knew that Banksy was a good man and, with the simplicity of an adolescent's thinking, I knew too that there had to be other fair-minded and decent British people like him.

10

Car Crashes & the End of an Era

I gave up goalkeeping abruptly in the summer of 1976, aged 20. Part of the reason was because I knew I was not going to grow beyond my 5 feet 7 inches. Furthermore, goalkeeping was never the same following Gordon Banks' premature retirement from English football – after losing his right eye in a near fatal car crash in October 1972. I could have filled a separate wallpaper book with press cuttings about the accident and yet, amazingly, I never kept one of them. It was, in truth, like a bereavement.

On 22nd October, 1972 my mother had called me into our sitting room to hear a newsflash on the BBC, which announced that the England goalkeeper had been seriously injured. I sensed the worst, especially when it was announced that his eyesight might be affected.

In later years I spoke to his Stoke City team-mate, former Republic of Ireland international, Terry Conroy, about how he learned the news of Banksy's accident and what affect it had had on the rest of the team.

TC, as he is still affectionately known at Stoke City, told

me that he and his wife Sue bought Banksy's old house at Loggerheads, near Market Drayton in Shropshire. They had just got married in May and knew that the Banks family were moving to a more private residence in the same area.

This meant that TC and Gordon Banks now travelled the same road, day in, day out, to the Victoria Grounds for training and matches. It was a round trip of 25 miles and the road was notorious in parts for bends and some very dangerous black spots.

On the day before the accident, Stoke City had played Liverpool at Anfield. Terry recalls, "Banksy was his usual brilliant self. He was spectacular and held Liverpool at bay for over an hour. The Liverpool Kop loved him. He always got a great reception at Liverpool."

During the game, Banks picked up an injury and he had to see the club physio the next day. After their Sunday lunch, TC and Sue were travelling into the Potteries when they saw Gordon's car completely smashed up and by the side of a fence. By then the emergency services and police had left the scene. Conroy says he couldn't believe what he was seeing and exclaimed to Sue, "That's Banksy's car!" It was, he recalls, an England World Cup sponsored Ford Consul.

"We didn't have mobile phones in those days so communications weren't instantaneous as they are today. By the time we reached the Potteries in the early afternoon, news was filtering through. There was a newsflash on the local radio and shortly afterwards it was all over the national news."

The next morning, the team gathered at the Victoria Grounds for training. All were in shock. "No exaggerating,"

Terry recalls, "we were in mourning. It was a gloom, like a heavy dark cloud had been draped over us. It was awful and so tragic. The team went to see him in hospital. We were stunned – in disbelief – that such a player, and a good person, should pick up an injury that could finish his career."

He continued, "Banksy was in his prime. The game against Liverpool the day before proved that. He would have gone on for another eight years, playing for Stoke and England. He had at least another 30 or 40 international caps in him. I've no doubt about that. He had no weight problems – he was lean and fit. That's probably what saved him."

It took a while for the team to settle after that. "Think about it," he says. "We had been robbed in '71 and '72 from two FA Cup Final appearances. Then we lost Banksy. The stuffing was knocked out of us."

TC recalls, "Tony Waddington was the eternal optimist. He didn't sign Peter Shilton until it was absolutely certain that Banksy wasn't going to recover sufficiently after the loss of his right eye. For eighteen months, we managed mainly with the help of our reserve goalkeeper, John Farmer, and Mike McDonald, bought from Clydebank for £20,000. In fairness, they did well. After losing Banksy, we finished fifteenth in the 1972-73 season."

The Republic of Ireland international continued, "Our real strength had been as a knock-out team. There wasn't a club in England who didn't fear us in a cup-tie. In the 1973-74 and 1974-75 seasons, our league form began to really pick up and both seasons we finished 5th from the top. In '74-75, we were leading the First Division [today's Premiership] at Easter. Then, in the last four games, we blew it and finished 5th, but just four points behind Derby

County, who won the Championship. The following season we were mid-table, but in the '76-77 season, we were relegated to the Second Division.

"I honestly don't think that would have happened if Banksy had still been playing. Why? We had a world-class replacement in Peter Shilton, no doubt about that. But, for several years, from 1968 onwards, until Gordon's car accident, we had an amazingly settled defence. Gordon and our back four – John Marsh, Denis Smith, Alan Bloor and Mike Pejic – were an incredible defensive force. They had built up a wonderful understanding. I have no doubt we could have become league champions, but fate deemed otherwise. Their relationship was built on consistency – week in and week out. They were ensconced. It also showed the loyalty they had to the club. That association began shortly after Banksy joined Stoke from Leicester in 1967."

Terry says it was amazing to see how hard Gordon Banks worked to try and regain his form. "We all felt sorry for him, but as the days went by our sorrow turned to abiding admiration. It was such a blow for him to deal with. Against many odds he had, with great dignity and determination, reached the top of his profession and, as his Stoke City team-mates, we all felt very proud and very privileged that he was one of us."

TC says that everyone at the club was hoping for a miracle, Tony Waddington above all. "But," he continues, "fate had dealt him insurmountable odds. Yet, undeterred, Banksy drew from those same unquenchable resources that he had been drawing on from his teenage years. He was determined to have another go. We could all see that."

Stoke's 'Wizard of the Wing' recalls travelling to Belgrade for a pre-season friendly around 1974, in which Gordon Banks played. "We lost 1-0 but he had a very good game. There were flashes of the old Banksy. But, ever the perfectionist regarding the art of goalkeeping, he felt he wasn't up to standard and shortly thereafter decided he wouldn't play competitively for Stoke again. That was sad, for we were all hoping he'd come back."

I too was hoping he would make a comeback. When eventually he did, in the North American Soccer League (NASL), it got little coverage on this side of the Atlantic. Effectively, Gordon Banks had become virtually invisible and only his closest friends, associates and old team-mates – like Terry Conroy – could fully appreciate the determination he was showing to play professional football again.

The End of a Dream

Banksy's car accident had been a major upset to me. But a bigger blow occurred in 1976, which, for a reason I still don't fully understand, caused me to give up goalkeeping and competitive football for good. Shaunie, my best friend, was killed in a multiple car crash in the summer of that year.

And the magic of our footballing dreams died with him.

He died late on the warm clear evening of August 22nd. I was almost 200 miles away in Co. Wicklow, helping Jim O'Hea on a camping holiday with the younger lads of Derry Athletic FC. The next day my parents came to bring me home for the funeral.

Shaunie was the eldest in his family and, more than anyone, his mother was dreading seeing me walk though the door, for Shaunie and me were like twins; she looked upon me as another son and I thought of her as a second mother.

She was sitting in the corner of the sitting room, in the same chair from which Shaunie had recognised the humanity of one of our enemy a few years earlier. The crowded room fell silent. We clasped one another sorrowfully. It was perhaps an hour before I could bring myself to go upstairs to his bedroom where he was being waked. The bunk beds in which we had laid and talked into the small hours about Gordon Banks and Pelé, and upon which we dreamed our dreams, had been removed to make room for his coffin.

It wasn't until the evening that the finality of his death suddenly impacted. I was keeping vigil over his remains, along with some of his younger brothers and sisters, neighbours and friends. Mourners were constantly coming to pay their last respects, when suddenly a gun battle between the IRA and the British Army erupted around the house. Instinctively, we all dived to the floor, panic electrifying the room. As I went down, I glanced back with concern for Shaunie. He was motionless. And then it hit me: "You really ARE dead!"

That was the moment I understood the magic had ended and my best friend would be no more.

In his autobiography *Banksy* (Penguin, 2003) Gordon Banks writes movingly about the death of his brother Jack:

'He was a great guy, a loving brother and we were all devastated at his passing. Nothing – home, family, business – was ever the same again. For the first time in my life I experienced the loss of a loved one. I grieved for months, mourned his loss for years and miss him to this day.'

That's exactly how my best friend's family and I felt and still feel about Shaunie almost four decades later. Often when I return home to Derry, I visit his grave. I've looked at the photograph on his headstone through the years: a handsome young man of twenty-one, wearing a football jersey, and smiling at me.

Across the decades I've watched his twenty-year-old best mate grow into middle age in the shiny reflection of his marble memorial. He now lies with his mother, father and younger brother, Pat. So many memories flash through my mind each time I go to pay my respects. Sadness has long passed when nowadays I visit their grave. I often smile with warmth, brought on by a deep sense of gratitude and love. And, as I walk away, I really do hope there is such a place as Heaven and that one day we might all be together again.

To Pelé's Homeland

Shaunie and I had often talked about travelling the world together. In 1972, we had hitchhiked around Ireland. In 1974, we hitchhiked across Normandy in France. We talked about visiting Brazil, the home of Pelé and, by then, owners of the Jules Rimet trophy after Brazil had won it three times.

In 1983-84, our dream was half-realised when I went to work there in the favelas of the twin cities of Olinda and Recife, in north-east Brazil, one of the poorest regions of the world. I worked with Irish nuns, priests and volunteers, whose commitment to the human rights of the poor was inspiring. I had also found my way there because of my mother, who was always conscientious and compassionate, and taught us the importance of caring for others. Her brother, Don, after whom I was named, was a priest in Peru.

On 9 October, 1983, I was walking along the magnificent beach of Boa Viagem ('Good Journey'), that stretches for miles to the south of the city of Recife. It was a Sunday afternoon and the beach was busy with sun worshippers.

I happened upon three young boys playing football on the golden sand. One was a talented little goalkeeper with superb agility, reflexes and handling. I sat unobtrusively on a nearby wall and enjoyed their fun. My mind was back in Derry and I thought of the days I too had spent with friends, especially Shaunie, doing exactly what these three young boys were doing. I wondered if the young goalkeeper had, as I had, an imagination set ablaze by a hero.

The whole setting brought with it waves of nostalgia. It was wonderful to contemplate from afar the happiest and most memorable days of my youth. That evening, when I returned to my room in Olinda, I sat with pen and paper and wrote the following reflection:

Goalkeeper

With illusions of grandeur
the young boy
leapt
high and low
in response to the shots
of his two friends.

Who was he
during those thrilling moments

on Boa Viagem beach?

Was he, perhaps,
Leao of Corinthians
Victor of Cruzeiro or
Neto of Santa Cruz?

Who would believe
that trying to catch an old ball
could be such fantasy
and fun?

Only he
who had once been
Jennings of Ireland
Yashin of Russia
and above all
Banks of England!

And, when I thought of Banks of England, I thought of Pelé of Brazil and, of course, 'That Save'. I thought too of 'That Save' I had made against Shaunie when I was twelve or thirteen that marked the beginning of our friendship, which began in innocence and carried us through some of the darkest days of modern Irish history.

We had lived through exceptional moments together; we faced what were for us epic choices about life and death, war and peace. At the same time, we lived in an era when sporting heroes were ordinary and unassuming people whose very modesty was the oxygen of dreams. And across the water, on a neighbouring island with whom we Irish had been in conflict for centuries, I had a hero who could fly. His name is Gordon Banks. From being a timid, fearful young boy, he taught me that impossible doesn't exist. Unknown to him, he helped save a young fan from making choices that had brought too much sorrow and sadness to Irish and British alike.

Who knows? Perhaps it was his best save ever.

11

Completing the Magic

Unexpected Encounters

During March 2004 I had an unexpected and exhilarating encounter on BBC Radio Stoke. Presenter Tim Wedgwood was interviewing me about *A Little Book of St. Patrick* (Columba Press, 2004), which I had just compiled. Having been alerted to my interest in Gordon Banks by a researcher, Wedgwood switched subjects and asked me about my hero's influence on my life. He then caught me by surprise a few minutes later when Gordon Banks came on the phone to join the conversation.

The unmistakable, soft-spoken Yorkshire accent asked, "How are you Don?"

I could tell by his warm response that he had been touched by my remarks. When Wedgwood asked him to respond to the impact he'd had on a young Irish boy during the 'Troubles', he replied, "It's wonderful. I just hope that now we have lots of peace between us all, that we don't see anymore of it... the killing and mayhem in Madrid shows how horrible it all is."

Before the encounter ended, I mentioned to Gordon that it was still one of my ambitions to have a photograph taken with him. He replied: "Anytime Don, anytime."

Conroy Connections

My son Carl was fourteen at the time of that radio interview – the age I was when my father took me to meet the world's greatest goalkeeper. Carl enjoys photography and so I determined that he would travel with me to Stoke City to complete for his dad the magic his grandfather helped create back in 1970.

I wrote to Banks shortly after our radio conversation to set up our meeting. In my initial enthusiasm I invited him and his wife to dinner. However, I sensed a hesitancy. He is, by nature, a shy man. His reply was courteous, but indicated that on the date I had suggested, he had to travel to Leicester and could only meet for the briefest moment. Circumstances intervened anyway and I had to sadly cancel the meeting. It seemed to me that the opportunity of meeting my boyhood hero had passed.

The following month I visited English artist Alan Damms in Sheffield. I had commissioned Alan to paint my favourite action shot of Gordon Banks, which was the cover of the first editon of this book. Alan, a lifelong and avid Sheffield United supporter, picked up my son Carl and me at the train station and drove us to Ferrars Road in the Tinsley area of Sheffield to see Gordon Banks' childhood home.

I found it very moving to stand in the street where my boyhood hero had once been a boy and where he himself had fantasised about his own hero, the great German goal-keeper, Bert Trautmann of Manchester City.

A few months later, as my wife Margaret and I were out for a walk one evening in Dublin, we met a friend, Mary Sweeney, and her husband, Paul Conroy. Before long Paul and I were discussing football and, inevitably, I mentioned Gordon Banks.

"My uncle played with Gordon at Stoke City," Paul informed me. "In fact, I saw him score the opening goal at Wembley when Stoke beat Chelsea in the 1972 League Cup Final."

"Terry Conroy is your uncle?" I asked, incredulously.

"Yes," Paul continued. "I met Gordon after the game and he said I must have been very proud to see my uncle score at Wembley. I was fourteen at the time."

A few days later Mary and Paul came to see my Gordon Banks memorabilia. Mary sat and carefully leafed through the scrapbook. At one point she commented: "I keep thinking of the love a little 12-year-old boy in the Creggan put into every page of this book."

How right she was. There is no other explanation, for I loved this man as the ancients must have loved their Gods. Every time I watched him play, heard his voice or saw his picture, my spirit soared. He awakened in me hope, purpose, commitment, imagination and self-esteem.

And now the meeting had become a possibility again!

Meeting Banks Once Again

On 18 March, 2005, Carl and I accompanied Paul Conroy and his brother Mark to Stoke-on-Trent. Their uncle had invited us to a dinner in Stoke City's Britannia Stadium at which Gordon Banks and Chelsea legend, the late Peter Osgood, were the guest speakers. The circumstances were ideal: I would be meeting my sporting hero in a relaxed environment with people who knew us both.

There was great excitement in our home the morning Carl and I left for England. Even though it was 5am when a taxi collected us for the airport, my wife Margaret and our daughters, Thérèse and Emma, all got out of their beds to wave us off. Terry Conroy picked us up at East Midlands Airport and drove us to Stoke-on-Trent.

Some had cautioned me that I might be disappointed when I met Gordon Banks again as an adult. I was reassured, however, by a comment Terry Conroy made during breakfast. "Gordon is a humble man," he said.

As the hours counted down to my second meeting with Banksy, I kept thinking of Shaunie and my father. Aware of my emotional state – for tears were inevitable – I began to worry that I might embarrass Gordon, and my son Carl.

We stayed at a wonderful family run establishment known as The Tollgate Hotel and Leisure in Blurton, Stoke-on-Trent, that was to be a home from home a few years hence. I didn't realise at the time that Adrian Oldfield, the son of the owners, was suffering the loss of his first little daughter, Eleanor May, who had died less than three weeks before. They were beautiful, kind and caring people and, whenever I return to Stoke, it is to the Tollgate Hotel and Leisure I go.

As I waited with Carl in the foyer of the Tollgate, I was listening to a selection of favourite songs that Adrian had compiled for the hotel background music system. I took a deep intake of breath when Simon and Garfunkle began to sing *Bridge over Troubled Waters*. This song had a very special and particular meaning to me regarding my best friend Shaunie.

I had discovered the music of Simon and Garfunkle in the mid-70s. The week before Shaunie died he collected me from training in his car and brought me home so I could shower (our changing rooms in 1976 at Oakland Park in the Creggan was an old steel lorry container within which were a couple of gymnasium benches. Showers were a rare luxury).

Shaunie had indicated earlier in the day that he wanted to talk to me about things that were worrying him. He had returned to Derry the year before from Edinburgh, where he had played for a short spell with Hibernians FC. He had left behind a sweetheart, Janet Henderson, for whom he retained very strong feelings. Janet was one of the reasons he wished to speak with me. Our plan was to drive across the border into neighbouring County Donegal and have dinner at a restaurant.

Before heading upstairs I put on Simon and Garfunkle and placed the needle of our old record player on the vinyl groove just before *Bridge Over Troubled Water*.

That's the last song I shared with Shaunie.

That evening, as we drove from Derry in the direction of Buncrana, we reached a place in the road where Lough Swilly becomes visible. Until then the road isn't particularly interesting and the sudden vista of the Lough, cradled by two hilly shorelines that seem to empty it into the north Atlantic, is a visual delight.

It was getting dark by the time we reached this point but

a full moon, rising above the far hills, illuminated the landscape with a magical light. The Lough reflected what appeared to be a golden finger that reached across it in our direction. It was so beautiful, we found a place to park and for the next three hours Shaunie poured out his heart and soul to me.

He told me things that were important he confided in a trusted friend, for there were important nuggets of information that I was able later to relate to loved ones, including Janet.

I still consider it uncanny to consider that just 200 yards from where we stopped before the rising moon, the accident occurred just one week later that claimed Shaunie's life.

As I stood in the Tollgate Hotel and listened to *Bridge Over Troubled Waters*, I felt an overwhelming sense of Shaunie's presence. Perhaps it was a coincidence, but I took comfort in the thought that my best friend was letting me know he was with me on this very special occasion when I would meet my boyhood hero again.

There He Was!

Terry had invited us to a small lounge so that the meeting would take place in relative privacy. As soon as we opened the door to it, there he was, sitting quietly, chatting and signing autographs for various items to be raffled later that evening during dinner.

Memories of Shaunie and my father were so vivid I could almost feel their presence. For ten minutes, while Gordon finished what he was doing, I stood with my back to him. I simply could not look at him without tears threatening.

Eventually, Terry Conroy beckoned and I turned to meet my boyhood hero. Elation, sadness and genuine gratitude overwhelmed me as I faced this unassuming Englishman. He was so much part of my fondest memories of my father, my family and my best friend. He was, in truth, a giver of hope.

For a full minute, I could not speak. Everyone with me, Paul, Mark and Terry Conroy, and my son Carl, knew how important, and how difficult, this moment would be. I spilled tears drawn from that well where the loss of loved ones is remembered with both gratitude and regret. My father and Shaunie were missing; yet I stood now with new friends and my own son. The hand that saved from Pelé had a firm grip of my own.

"I'm sorry Gordon," I said, "I knew this would happen." He smiled and reassuringly tapped me on the shoulder.

"It's okay," he responded.

When eventually I regained control, my first words were 'Thank you'. In truth, there was nothing more I needed to say. Carl and I appreciated the sensitivity of the Conroys, who retreated to allow Banks and me time to share some moments together. He asked if I had liked his book *Banksy* and, when I told him I especially liked his childhood memoirs, he spoke about the hardships endured by his mother.

"I can still see her putting the family washing through an old hand-operated wringer in our kitchen before hanging it out on the line." As he recalled this, I could see my own mum doing similar tasks back in Derry.

We looked through my scrapbook together. I pointed out his prized autograph and we laughed together at what I had discovered a few days earlier. On page 200, behind a large photograph of himself gathering a ball during a training session prior to the Mexico World Cup, I was surprised to discover, in my childish handwriting, the prayer: 'Please God Help England Win the World Cup'. An Irish boy's 1970 aspiration written at a time when attitudes were softer. I had shown it to Terry Conroy earlier who, with a wink and a chuckle, commented: "Don't worry Don, your secret's safe with me. I won't tell!"

Roles Reversed

What I loved most about our second meeting was the way he related to my son, Carl.

"How are you young man?" he asked. He then asked him if he had a favourite sport. "It doesn't matter how good you are. It's important just to get out into the fresh air and get exercising."

Watching, in my opinion, the greatest goalkeeper of all times interact with my boy, brought me back to that 2nd August day in 1970 when he showed me the same respect and kindness. In his presence I could see Carl grow in stature, as I too had done. I couldn't help but think of how my parents must also have cherished this good man for the same respect he showed their boy, almost 35 years ago.

"I can see Dad why you liked Gordon Banks so much," Carl commented later that night when we returned to our room at the Tollgate Hotel. "He wasn't only a great goal-keeper, but he's a really nice person. I couldn't believe how ordinary and down-to-earth he is." Then, with a giggle and a mischievous twinkle in his eyes, he threw me some bait.

"If I had lived in the olden days, he would have been my hero too!"

I swallowed it and dived across the room, and the two of us wrestled on top of his twin bed. "I'll show you who's the 'old man'," I said, as we collapsed onto the floor in a heap of laughter. It was a perfect ending to another never-to-be-forgotten day.

'My Greatest Fan'

I got that longed for photograph with my boyhood hero, taken by my son. As I looked into the lens of Carl's camera, I could see his grandfather, who had died before he was born.

It still amazes me how my father had weaved this piece of magic. He was an ordinary man with no influence in either civil society or the sporting world. Gordon Banks was, in August 1970, an English icon. He was a World Cup Winner, recipient of the OBE, and 'That Save' against Pelé, less than two months earlier, had established him as the greatest goalkeeper in the world. Undaunted, my father was driven by a simple faith that if only he could make this happen, it would be important for his boy. Never once in his life did he tell me he loved me and, yet, that moment had everything. It injected real hope and hunger for improvement in my life. In it I found myself and never looked back.

Throughout my adult life, because I worked in the field of human rights and also as a journalist, I have had the opportunity to meet many notable personalities of the 20th Century. These include people like: Rosa Parks, Kim Phuc, Mother Teresa, His Holiness the Dalai Lama, Pope John Paul II, Archbishop Desmond Tutu, President Clinton, and pop stars like Mick Jagger, Bono and Bob Geldof. But nothing, absolutely nothing, other than an audience with God, will ever surpass the pure joy my father gave me as a boy – the day we met Gordon Banks!

At the lounge, Gordon had gone off to mingle with many of his old Stoke City team-mates who had come to town for the occasion. Before we left, he came back to me.

"You asked me to sign your book so let's do it now," he said.

I gave him my copy of his autobiography *Banksy*. He opened it on the title page and wrote:

> *To Don*
> *Good Luck To My Greatest Fan*
> *Gordon Banks*

My Greatest Fan! – a young boy inside me swelled with pride!

Part II

The Footballer & The Man
An Interview with Gordon Banks

On Tuesday 22 November, 2005, I was heading to Stoke-on-Trent again with my son Carl, this time to interview my boyhood hero. I was thrilled Banksy had agreed to be interviewed for this book. His daughter Wendy insisted on collecting us from East Midlands Airport and, with her partner Andy, returning us the following day.

Close now to seventy, Gordon Banks is no longer the powerful athlete of his prime, but his presence still turned people's heads as we made our way to begin our interview. At one time, Banks was an untouchable deity. Indeed, the day my father took me to meet him, my only expectation was to marvel from the terraces. Now, 35 years later, I discovered something important and profound.

Experience has taught Gordon Banks that applause and adulation all too quickly pass – even for the greatest – and that in life there are constants that ground us and connect us to our humanity. In the interview that follows, Gordon

Banks speaks the names of icons who once were, like himself, global superstars. Yet, when he speaks of Ursula, his German wife and best friend, we encounter the heart of a good man who was blessed with a wonderful lifelong companion.

Empty stadiums are cold and eerie places where net-less goalposts seem naked. When momentous sporting moments are but echoes in our minds, they are best savoured with family and close friends. Gordon Banks learned these values in his childhood home and, no doubt, therein lies the greatness of this extraordinary man who refused to forget his origins and those who loved him most.

It's what makes him a giant over the suits that control football today and who have, to varying degrees, robbed the game of its very soul.

The Interview

DON MULLAN: Do you remember the young Irish boy from 1970 with the scrapbook in Co. Donegal, before the game against Finn Harps? Alex Elder was there with you.

GORDON BANKS: Alex, full back, the Irish lad, yes. I can remember the game but I can't remember the actual happening. We always had people that would come up and ask for autographs, photographs and, like you, young boys who were goalkeepers. Hopefully, I would always be the type of person that would try to help somebody because I knew that when I was a young boy there was no help whatsoever. I realised that young boys with their fathers, who came to me, wanted to learn a little bit about how I was doing it. So, if I could pass on a tip, I was always happy to do that.

What's your earliest goalkeeping memory?
My earliest memory is going to school with friends and the first thing that we tended to do was to kick things. It didn't matter what it was: a tin can, a stone, anything kickable. When we were able to find a tennis ball, or any sort of a ball, that was a bonus.

Most of the time it finished up on the roof and I'd often

be the one who'd have to climb up to retrieve it. But the beauty about that was when I was on the roof there would often be five or six balls that had never been retrieved. That was always a happy time for us. There really was little else for us to do. There was radio, obviously, but no television; so we were outside and the only thing we could do was either play cricket or football.

From a goalkeeping perspective, even though I was very young, I was seeing the ball come towards me and my eyes began picking up the speed of the ball, sending a message to the brain – it's going here, it's going there – and so I'd move in anticipation. I know now this was improving my reflexes.

As I got a little bit older, we started to play lots and lots of five-a-side football games in the park. The only other sport I played, after I began to earn a bit of money doing a paper round, was tennis.

I wasn't a bad outfield player and was eventually selected for the school team as a centre half. But I sometimes played as goalkeeper. The teacher said to me one day, "Gordon, you can't play in two positions; you will have to decide which position you want to concentrate on." I asked him which position we were weakest in, thinking that I could help the school team. He said "Goalie", so I said I would play in goal.

After half a season, I was asked to go for a trial with Sheffield Boys and was selected. I didn't do too badly in the first game. I think it was after the fourth or fifth game he dropped me from the first team. I was still in the squad but I was left sitting on the bench. So me dad said, "I'd let you stay at school son if you had been in the first team and playing, but since you're on the bench, I'm afraid at Christmas you'll have to leave school and get some work for the family. I can't have you just sitting around," – which was quite right.

And tell me about your family?
My family had very little. There were four boys. My father worked at the Steel Foundry then he had to come out because of his chest – it was full of smoke and, like everybody at the time, he and my mother smoked. We were a very poor family so each brother had to leave school early to get a job. Our Jack, the eldest, he worked as an accountant. My brother, David, was a bricklayer and Michael was on the railway as a stoker. They were all bringing a wage in which helped pay for food and household expenses.

Our Jack had a bone marrow disease. His bones were very brittle and I think he had something like twelve or fifteen operations on his legs, so they were all scarred and he never grew. After his operations we had to push him around in a wheelchair and then he was on sticks. All the time he seemed to have accidents. I remember playing in the backyard of our house with him one day with a tennis ball. It was only a tiny little yard and he just fell on the ground and said, "You'd better fetch the ambulance." He couldn't get up because his legs had broken.

What's your fondest memory of your mum?
My fondest memory of my mother is that, regardless of what little she had, it would go to feed us. She had very few luxuries. My father wasn't earning a lot of money and they had to keep four boys. Lots of times it would be bread and

jam and stew, if she could get some meat. But, whatever she had in her purse, it would go to make sure her family was all right. That's my fondest memory of my mother. She was a very, very hard working person. For example, in those days there was the old dolly tub where they used to scrub clothing in the water and then put it through the mangle and hang them out to dry. She had a very hard, very tough life because my dad was in and out of work with his health.

Your fondest memory of your father?

My fondest memories are of him encouraging me to keep progressing as best I could – to keep trying and not give in. Like, for example, when I once let in twelve goals during a trial. He said, "Well forget that now, just carry on and keep trying to improve." Dad encouraged me a tremendous amount.

Weren't your first jobs tough and dirty although, unwittingly, the hard work was preparing you for the future?

I left school at Christmas, just short of my 15th birthday. O-Levels or A-Levels weren't going then, so I didn't have any academic qualifications. Dad got me a job with a coal merchant he met in a workingmen's club where he drank. The guy would employ young boys leaving school for the first year, pay them next to nothing, sack them after a year and then get another one coming out of school. It was cheap labour, but I didn't mind because it was a job and I was earning two or three quid a week to help the family.

It was really hard work. First, a coal wagon would come in, empty its load onto a steel plate hammered onto the wooden floor, and then the shovelling began, filling bag after bag. He'd then stand on the lorry and I'd have to lift the heavy bags up for him to stack. Once the lorry was loaded we started our deliveries around Sheffield.

The upside of all this shovelling, lifting and carrying the heavy weights, was the building of the upper part of my body. Mind you, I was so tired and hungry at the end of the day.

My brother David got me a job doing hard manual labour on a building site: digging ditches for the drains, mixing concrete for the foundations, unloading lintels. It didn't pay much but, then again, it was also strengthening the upper part of my body.

How did your professional career begin?
To get some overtime, I would work early Saturday morning until lunchtime, earning double time. I'd then rush home, wash and change very quickly, and shoot into Sheffield to watch Wednesday or United play. I loved to see them play.

One Saturday I got home, washed and changed but, having missed the bus, I realised I wasn't going to get to a game on time. So, I decided to watch a game at the local recreational ground, near where I lived. I was leaning on the fence when a bloke approached me and said, "You used to play in goal for Sheffield Boys, didn't you?" He asked me if I wanted a game as the goalie for his team, Millspaugh Steelworks, hadn't turned up. I said yes I'd play and ran home to get my football boots and socks. I had no shorts, so I played in my working trousers and they loaned me a green shirt. After the game, the coach asked if I wanted to play regularly. "We never know when this guy is going to come," he said. I told him, "Yes, I'll play," and that's when it all started.

I later went for a trial at a club called Rawmarsh Welfare, which played in the Yorkshire League, a much better league. I let twelve in and went back to playing for Millspaugh. Then, near the end of the season, Chesterfield offered me a trial with one of their junior teams. There were only six games left and they told me that if I did okay they'd have me back for the next season. Although I missed out on two years at Chesterfield because I was sent to Germany on National Service.

And that's where you met your wife, Ursula?
That's right. I was stationed in Germany and the camp was in the middle of nowhere. There was a guesthouse on the hill and it had a bar, then further down was the town, Königslutter. I was in the Royal Signals and we were monitoring Soviet communications.

I first saw Ursula in the bar and I just couldn't keep my eyes off her because she was so attractive; I really did fancy her. She worked in a ladies shop in Königslutter, where she lived. I called to see her a short time after and we went out dancing. That's when our friendship started.

How did your parents feel about you falling in love with a German girl and bringing her back? Because of the recent war with Germany, was there a stigma perhaps?
No, I think that had died down by then. I think my mother just expected me to be courting an English girl. Although she didn't know Ursula at the time, believe me, my mother

really did get to love her a lot when she came over and appreciated what a super woman she really is.

Where did your self-belief come from?
My father taught me the importance of sticking up for myself. "You have to fight your own battles and you have to get on with life, whatever is thrown at you," he told me. He was that type of man himself, so I think that was borne through him. He was a bit of a tough sort of person and I think it rubs off on children.

I was quiet but determined and, because I had worked hard at the jobs that I had, I started to work hard being a goalkeeper. You would not believe the hours that I spent going back in the afternoons once I signed as a professional with Chesterfield. All the rest had finished at lunchtime. I would have something to eat and then I would be back practising with either the apprentices or reserve players. Later on, it was some of the first team players that were trying to knock balls past me. That even happened at Leicester on a Sunday morning. It amazed me that first team players would want to come back for extra training. And, of course, that improved my goalkeeping because these guys were pretty accurate. My father gave me this determination – "Don't ever give in, stick at it and get to the top".

Perhaps, in a strange kind of way, people like your Leicester City manager, Matt Gillies, actually helped to bring the best out of you when, in 1967, he suggested your best days were over and you should move on.
I think you might be right; he might have done, yes. I knew

my career hadn't finished. He said, "I think I've had the best out of you Gordon; what do you think about leaving?" I said, "Well, if that's what you think of me then, yes, I will." I thought to myself, 'I don't want to stay at a club that doesn't appreciate what I'm doing. I can go to one that does.' Although I was disappointed, I suppose it did make me a lot more aggressive to do well.

In moving to Stoke City, as well as finding a club, you found a home.
That's right! The feeling here with the fans was fantastic. The Manager, Tony Waddington, was a lovely guy who mixed with the players and tried to help them with any difficulties they had. The Directors were superb. They would come and speak to you, tell you jokes, have a laugh with you, get you a drink after the game, and that sort of thing; it was completely different.

And Stoke City, especially Tony Waddington, repaid your loyalty to the club after your car accident in October, 1972. Did you find yourself grieving within for the end of your career?
Not at that moment, no. Not at that early stage. After a few months, I was actually back training. I started to train with the lads and then, one day, it went and from that day on I never saw anything ever again with my right eye. The light went out.

Then I was shattered. I realised that I would never play again at the level I had reached.

To be honest, I didn't think I was ever going to play again. I honestly thought my playing career was over. God bless him, Tony Warrington, offered me a coaching job with the youth team, which I grabbed because I so badly wanted to stay in the game. As it happened, Stoke City had seven apprentices, but no goalkeeper. So, when I took them training I would go into goal during the shooting session. In the early months the ball just flew past me. I would try to catch it and it would slip through my hands; it was hitting me on the face and everything. But, as the months went by, my good eye now began picking up the speed of the ball and soon they were having difficulty in getting it past me.

Amazingly, you then decided to make a comeback in the North American Soccer League.
Yes, in 1976, I got an offer to go to America, which I took. I was playing but I'm absolutely terrified thinking, 'What have I done coming here?' Though in practice I was doing okay. I was still agile and getting around, even though the surface in Miami was very hard. Then we started playing competitive games and I couldn't believe it because I could still read the game well. It was a pretty good standard, like the old Second Division or today's Championship. The first season I was there we won our league. I couldn't believe it! We actually won our league and we had only got Ian Callaghan, I think, besides myself, who was a fairly well-known player. The other teams, like New York's Cosmos, had players like Pelé, Beckenbauer and Carlos Alberto, and we beat them on points; although, in the play-offs they beat us. I couldn't believe how well I had done.

After the accident I received many letters of support from friends and fans, which was very important. Once in America, and doing well, I began to receive letters from people, mothers especially, asking me to write a word of encouragement to a child or someone in a similar situation. It was wonderful to be able to write and say I'm playing football again and after America to write and say I'm playing golf, and you too will be able to do all these things. It was great for me to be able to do that.

You were in your mid-twenties by the time you made your full international debut.
That's right. I played for the England under-23 team, but I was 25 when I got my first full cap. But I didn't sign professional forms until I was 20. It was quite early in my career, but late for someone who had started straight from school at 16, which I hadn't done.

How did your parents feel when you were selected for England?
Proud as hell.

Were they at the World Cup Final in 1966?
God yes! All of them were absolutely proud as punch, especially Mam and Dad and Our Jack.

Was Jack at it?
Oh yes. He was there. He was very proud.

I can see you had a great love for Jack.
Oh yes. He was a lovely man, he really was. He could mix with anybody. He was a very friendly person and people would take to him. He made a tremendous amount of friends. He really did make a lot of friends. Smashing guy.

Probably the happiest memory I have of the family was each time Our Jack came out of hospital, hoping that he was going to be alright again and having a little homecoming for him.

When did you first begin to dream about a football career?

When Chesterfield took me on for a trial, when they said they'd like me to play in the last six games for their youth team.

I did alright playing for the youth team and they pushed me into the A Team, which played in a better league. The players were all a lot older than me. I was still only about 16 and all these other guys were 19, 20, 21 and 22 in this league. I got shoved into the reserves at the age of just 17 and this was where I really began learning the art of goalkeeping.

No club had a goalkeeping coach on its staff. The trainer and physio – if they had a physio – would all be outfield players. The physio would train the lads and he would look after the injuries and sprains. They had a doctor, obviously, but he would only be there on match days.

So, once I got into the Central League side, I now had to learn very quickly. And I had to do it myself, because there was no goalkeeping coach.

One thing I did learn at Chesterfield, and I never saw this at any other football club at the time, was how to work a boxers' punch ball. The trainer taught me how to use it. My! That didn't half help me with timing. It was fantastic for timing. I learned to do all the things a boxer would do and even began doing tricks. It was all about timing, which was essential with high crosses. So when I was jumping for a cross the timing was dead right, especially when I had to punch. That was the only thing really, which helped me as a goalkeeper during training in those days.

But playing in the Central League side, where half the team was semi-pros, we were playing the likes of Man United in front of a crowd of 15,000 people at Old Trafford. They had players like Bobby Charlton; they were all full-time players, so you can imagine what it was like. So I was quickly having to learn the art of goalkeeping. When a goal got past me I would always analyse what had happened. Maybe I should have been a little bit over there; maybe I should have come off my line a little bit more. I was always thinking about these things because I didn't want to lose my place. I felt like a professional player. Oh! It was great. I loved it – especially playing in front of the big crowds.

Who was the greatest influence on your career?
Probably my family; my Father was always pushing me on. He'd always say, "If you let a bad goal in, you have to push it to the back of your mind and you have to focus on the next shot that's going to come."

My brothers gave me lots of encouragement as well. Michael and David had played for the school team. While they didn't go on to progress in football, they would be urging me to get there. They were the biggest influence, without any question.

The other people who influenced me were the two Sheffield goalkeepers. Ted Burgin of Sheffield United was one, and a lad called McIntosh who played for Sheffield Wednesday. I would always stand behind the goal and watch where they stood, what they did.

The goalkeeper I admired most at that time was Bert Trautmann* who played for Manchester City and, funnily enough – I would have been about 16 or 17 at the time – I actually played against him which, to me, was like, "Oh crikey, I can't believe I'm on the same pitch!"

Did you ever tell him he was one of your heroes?
Oh yes, I did. I told him. I said to him, "I used to watch you and I think you are a great goalkeeper." I remember his reply. He said, "Well, you keep working and trying hard and you'll get there." He was a lovely man.

How important was Ursula in your career?
She was fantastic. When the babies came along she was such a dedicated mother. There was no way she would allow me to feed them in the middle of the night. She would always get up. She never insisted "It's your turn", as she wanted to make sure I got the rest I needed before training the next day. She was fantastic; she has always been a wonderful wife to me and a wonderful mother to the children. She was absolutely dedicated to being a great housewife, woman, friend, companion and mother. When I had the accident, Ursula, more than anyone, held our family together and saved me from falling apart.

Apart from the accident, what was the lowest moment in your career?
Apart from my accident, when I was playing here with Stoke City in two Semi-Finals of the FA Cup in 1971 and '72. The first was probably a lot worse than the other. I was

captain of the side at the time. Stoke had never played in an FA Cup Final in over 100 years, nor have they to this day. I have rarely said this about a referee, but I just felt we had been totally robbed. Both games were against Arsenal. In the first game at Hillsborough in 1971, we were winning 2-0 at half time and really outplaying them. In the second half, fair enough, they got a perfectly good goal. Nobody could complain with that. But then, for some reason – I still don't know why – everything seemed to be destined by the referee to go Arsenal's way.

Hillsborough has a big clock and I could see it was something like seven minutes into injury time. The trainer had only been on maybe twice at the very most. In those days, they used to get the sponge, splash it over the injured player, get him on his feet and then go off the field. I could see people leaving the stand and I couldn't believe the ref was letting the match continue. I'm thinking, 'blow the whistle!' when Arsenal came down the field. Mike Pejic and an Arsenal player go for a 50/50 ball. Both fall down but the ref gives a free kick to Arsenal between the edge of our box and the touchline.

Arsenal always did the same thing with their free-kicks. Once the ball was struck they would pull out leaving the space for an attacker to run in and meet the header. I knew this and was saying to myself, 'If I get this ball the game is over – it's got to be over!'

So the ball is knocked into the space and I came and got a good clean catch with both hands. Next thing I know, John Radford is into the middle of my neck and my back. Bang! Of course, I've now dropped the ball and there was an almighty scramble. I'm thinking, 'This is a free-kick without any question; the game is finished. It's a free kick for us – it's got to be!' But, no, the ref let play continue and the ball went out for a corner kick.

From the resulting corner – and this is taking another minute or two at least – the ball comes in. I don't know who it was, bang, the ball is going right inside the post and John Mahoney handballs it. They get a penalty and score. We only had time for kick-off and the ref blew the whistle for full-time. 2-2.

That literally killed our team. We had four young lads, John Mahoney, Mike Pejic, Terry Conroy and John Marsh, who had never been to a final. They were in the dressing room and were literally crying because this idiot had robbed us. I used to think a referee would never do that in a game, but I really felt we had been robbed. Sometimes, when supporters would complain, I'd laugh it off but in this game the ref really did rob us.

In my scrapbook, I have a photograph of you from that game and you are really angry.
I was. I was livid. I had a right go at him coming off the field. I pointed to the clock. I said, "Look at the time; we never had the trainer on." I said, "You've been diabolical." Of course, we couldn't recover in the replay. We lost 2-0 or something. There was no way we were going to recover from that. It was alright for me because I had played in an FA Cup Final, but, these lads, they never went on to play in one and that was sad because they should have been there.

And what about the other Semi-Final?
We played Arsenal again in 1972 at Everton's Goodison

Park. It was nearly as bad. This is a true story; you can ask any supporter around here and they'll tell you. Again we were beating them 1-0. Arsenal's John Radford raced after a through ball on the right wing. I will never forget it because he must have been a good 10 yards offside. The linesman, however, just carries on and does nothing. I'm thinking, 'He can't!' but he does.

Anyway, John Radford pulls the ball back and knocks it into the back of the net. That's the equalizing goal. Half our team chased the linesman and guess what he said after the game? He said, "The ice cream seller was wearing the same as the Stoke colours [all white] and I thought he was a Stoke player." True story! I am not exaggerating. I swear to God! 1-1.

Their other goal – now listen to this – this is a true story also, I'm not exaggerating. I don't know who their player was, but Stoke's Peter Dobing was a centre forward who had come back for a corner kick. He was only just inside the box and he jumps up with this other guy and both of them did exactly the same movement, Peter heads it clear and the ref gives a penalty! They don't even fall down. Nothing! We're stunned. We couldn't believe it. We could not believe the decisions. Anyway, that's football. But they were my most disappointing moments.

Your greatest save?
It's always hard to pick because I played a lot of matches. The Pelé save, obviously, has got to be one. It's up there in the top three. You need to look at it because of who it was, because of the awkwardness of what I had to do to just get my hand to it. It wasn't dropping alongside my dive. It was

bouncing a couple of yards in front of me, so I had to anticipate how high it's going to come up from the hard surface to just get my hand to it. That was the hardest part of the save and, also, the agility to get from the centre of the goal over to the right post.

The other couple? The penalty save against Geoff Hurst in the Semi-Final of the League Cup. A lot of the fans pick that one out because it got us to the final. Geoff had scored in the first leg with a penalty and, in a roundabout way, he gave it away really because he did exactly the same thing as when he scored at Stoke. On that occasion I got my hand to it. I had pushed it into the side netting but it was a goal. But he did exactly the same thing on the second occasion! He placed the ball down and his run was from maybe six or seven yards outside the penalty area. So he just pounded up and hit it with all his might. I'm thinking, 'He can't change now, coming at this speed, he's got to hit it to my right, like he did with the first one.' I am starting to go and, then, he got his foot a little bit more underneath the ball. So, as I'm leaping across now – I have anticipated – it's now rising up so I've got to bring my right hand up and drag it behind the ball. It tipped my hand and that one spun over the bar.

Yeah! When you make a penalty save it's always a good save, but the speed he hit that ball!

There was another one. Denis Law chipped a ball at Wembley when he was playing for Scotland. He got through the England defence and I had come out. He saw me off my line and chipped the ball. He lifted it over me, so I had to back pedal. The hardest thing to do is to run backwards and push upwards. But as I pushed upwards I also had to dive backwards and claw it away from the goal.

And there was another one, against Newcastle United, here at Stoke. One person, Stan, came up to me and said, "I remember a better save than Pelé's. I was standing behind the goal."

It wasn't the Boothen End; it was the other end at the old Victoria Ground. Wyn Davies was the Newcastle centre forward attacking from their left, my right hand side. The ball had been driven quite firmly so I couldn't come for the cross. It was about eight or ten yards out and Wyn was running to meet it. I could see the way he was heading it that he was going to push it to my right. So, again, I anticipated a little bit and started moving. But, he hit it right towards the top corner. Because I'd started, I got my weight moving quickly, pushed up, just got a fingertip to it and pushed it over the bar. Only people in the ground will remember that one – especially those behind the goal, like Stan, because they could see the speed and impact of it as they were so close. That probably was one of the best saves I ever made.

What are the highlights of your career?
I think the start of it all has to have been the biggest thrill for me. Getting that chance, that lucky break. Missing that bus into Sheffield for a United or Wednesday game and that team being without a goalie. If it wasn't for that goalie not turning up, I probably wouldn't be talking to you today. Had that not happened God only knows what I would have done.

Then, of course, climbing the ladder. Getting the chance with Chesterfield, even though it was a third division side. It didn't matter one iota to me because – I still say it to this day – any player that plays in any league will get as much pleasure on a Saturday afternoon as I did playing in the First Division, or Premiership as it is now. It's the thrill of getting changed in the dressing room; the thrill of being with your mates; the thrill of running out onto the field and afterwards having a joke in the shower or the bath, and having a drink with the lads. It's that lovely feeling that you get as a team.

Then, of course, having the break to go to Leicester City. This, I think, is when I really had an opportunity of beginning the hard work.

I didn't know at the time that it was going to lead to all these bigger things. All I knew was that I wanted to improve my goalkeeping: going down and holding the ball, getting a hold of crosses, coming out, timing my run, getting the angle right. This was really where I think the real hard work was done. I did it myself and then, even when we got a coach for goalkeepers, I would tell him what I wanted: short work, long work, crosses, etc. And he obliged, which was good of him.

What about other highlights?

The other highlight was, of course, when I was awarded the OBE and going to Buckingham Palace with my family. We could only take two children. Mind you, the other one, Julia, was a baby anyway. Robert and Wendy went with us and that was a fantastic day – a fabulous day.

Tony Waddington had got the Stoke Chairman to lay on his Rolls Royce to take us from the hotel and through the gates of the palace. The Queen was away when I got my OBE. It was the Queen Mother who officiated. "What did she say to you?" I was asked. Sometimes she doesn't speak to everybody, but I recall there was a guy with her and, as you came along, he leaned forward to tell her something about the person receiving the Award. The Queen Mother looked at me and asked: "How did you cope with the heat in Mexico during the World Cup?"

When people talk of you as the greatest goalkeeper of all times, how do you feel?

It's nice that people say that. You feel nice about it. But in the back of your mind you say to yourself, it's impossible for anybody to know who is the best. Because they can't be in every country at once; they can't see every goalkeeper playing. So, it's just a matter of conjecture.

Who were, in your opinion, the greatest goalkeepers you ever encountered?

Oh, Lev Yashin of Russia was a fantastic goalkeeper. I used to think we were a bit similar in that he tried to make goalkeeping look as easy as he possibly could. Not make it acrobatical when you didn't have to. He did straightforward goalkeeping. His angles were excellent; he would come for crosses; he would command his area; he would organise his defence.

He had all the attributes. He would punch when he had to punch, catch the ball when he had to catch it. For me, he did everything right – a great goalkeeper.

Another one I thought was very similar was Pat Jennings. He was a terrific goalkeeper. He had huge hands. I remember he used to catch the ball with one hand in the air and pull it down. His positioning was excellent. He really was a terrific goalkeeper.

In a modern day context, Peter Schmeichel was an excellent goalkeeper. One advantage he had, which made him such an excellent one-on-one opponent, was that he used to be an ice hockey goalkeeper. They used to make stars of themselves when the guy was shooting to cover as much of the goal as possible. He was excellent on one-on-one – the best I've ever seen. But, not only that, he was very agile for a big man, about 6ft 4 and very athletic. He could get across the goal and would command his area, very much a Yashin feature. His angles were good. And, in my time, there were also a lot of good English goalkeepers – excellent English goalkeepers.

I'd love to hear your thoughts on those you consider to be among the best footballers. What about Bobby Moore?
Oh! I played with and against some great players. Bobby Moore was one of the greatest players I played behind. He was an absolutely wonderful player. You couldn't really go anywhere and find a better centre half than Bobby. He was such a graceful player. He didn't have to be physical because he could read the game so well. He could see an opponent making a move out of the corner of his eye and immediately Bobby was on his way to intercept him and take the ball away.

He hardly ever gave a pass away. He was a terrific player and I had the confidence to throw the ball to him every time because I knew he would keep us in possession.

Bobby, as I said, was a gentleman. He was a dapper man, always immaculately dressed, whether it was casual or going to a dinner. It would be the most modern, cleanest shirt and matching tie, immaculate suit; in training, his gear always seemed to fit better than everybody else's. He was absolutely dapper and a good leader. He led by his own play. He dominated and would be confident in what he was doing, and would want you to do the same – "Come on Banksy, come on so and so," you know? It was so sad when he died. So sad.

Alf Ramsey?

Lovely man! Best manager I have ever played under. An absolutely fantastic guy. He was so thorough about everything he did. Like, for example, the England set up for Mexico. He took the 1968 Olympic dossier and examined it before we went out there. What Olympic athletes did to acclimatise to the high altitude was they went higher to train and when they came to a lower altitude they found the breathing easier. So that's exactly what he did.

We did a weeks training in Mexico City. And I'll tell you – I couldn't believe it – just carrying a couple of bags from the bus to our hotel rooms, only a short distance, we were panting. We thought, 'Crikey, we've got to run in this!' Anyway, we had a week's training, which we found very hard. Then we went to Bogotá in Columbia and Quito in Ecuador, trained up there, played two International friendly matches, came back down and now it was was easier to run around.

Your second International game for England was against Brazil. A real baptism of fire!

It was, yes. My first was against Scotland at Wembley on 6th April, 1963. Brazil and then the Rest of the World were the next two. We played the Rest of the World in October '63, a FIFA selection because it was the 100th Anniversary of the English Football Association. We played them at Wembley and we won 2-0. I was delighted about that given the quality of the opposition. I'll tell you who played in that game: Lev Yashin of Russia, Santos of Brazil, Eusebio of Portugal, Denis Law and my auld enemy Jim Baxter of Scotland. Pelé was there too and Spain's Puskas and Gento Lopez. What a side; they had a fantastic team. Who was the French winger? Can't remember his name [Raymond Kopa], fabulous player, terrific game!

Did you know that up until your accident you played in 75% of the England games that Alf managed?
Did I?

As your own career was terminated prematurely because of the accident, when you had 73 caps, it's probable you would have been the first England goalkeeper to reach the 100 mark.
I had a chance of doing that. I think so. When I look back at the stats, they were surprising. I honestly have never been one for remembering how many clean sheets I had or how many wins I had with England, until just before my autobiography was published. When somebody actually showed me, I was surprised at some of the stats of what I had achieved, which was very pleasant.

And what about Pelé?
Without any question, he was the greatest player that I have seen – without any question. People talk about Maradona

and people like Henry and some of today's other great players. But Pelé could do everything – and well. As good as Jimmy Greaves could score; as good as George Best could dribble through players; as good as Bobby Charlton could hit the ball from 35yards – he could do everything, headers included. He could do everything at the top level and I have never seen another as good as him. I would love to think that before I die I will see one who could do everything like he could. But, so far, there has not been anyone as good as him. He was fantastic.

And what a compliment that he considers you to be the greatest goalkeeper.
Yes. I was amazed at that because, with Santos, they went on tours all around the world and he played against virtually every goalie. So, yes, it was a nice compliment.

Pelé was a great player and a great sportsman as well. I've never ever seen him kick anybody in retaliation. He got kicked loads of time, kicked lumps out of, but he never retaliated. He just got on with his game and tried to show his opponents up a little bit more if he could. A great sportsman!

One of the great images is of him going up to Bobby Moore and swapping jerseys after the 1970 clash in Mexico. It's iconic!
Yes. Bobby had a great game that day. His timing and his tackling was absolutely 100%.

And England didn't deserve to lose that day. A draw would have been a fairer result.
Yes, I agree. In fact we created the game's better chances.

Alan Ball hit the bar.

And Jeff Astle missed that sitter, a complete sitter. But, that's football; you can't legislate, can you? You don't know what's going to happen.

And George Best who, sadly, as we speak, is gravely ill?
[George Best died on 25 November 2006, three days after this interview.]

George! An absolutely magical player – absolutely magical. Somebody told me a story about him – I'm sure this was in Ireland before he came over. Someone would tell him, perhaps his dad, to get a ball and to run with it, touching it with both feet – inside and outside – as many times as he could. Running slowly at first, then quicker, a bit quicker and quicker again. So much so that, by the time he came over here, you would have thought that ball was tied to his bloody shoelace.

And that's what he could do. He could keep control of the ball at amazing speeds. He also had this wonderful aptitude of waiting until a defender was about to make a tackle. He'd know the guy was about to lunge and he'd push the ball, ride the tackle and off he'd fly towards the goal. Next, the defender would try to bring him down because he can't afford to let George free, but still he could ride the tackle and stay on his feet while the defender is on the floor, out of the game. He had the ability to carve a huge opening, get clean through and kill the defence. I've never seen a player able to do that as well as George. It was absolutely fantastic.

He scored a goal down here at Stoke. I've got a frame of it at home – he had three of us going, two defenders and me, with just the movement of his body. George was on the edge of the box and Willie Morgan, Manchester United's right winger, a slim lad, drove the ball across to him. He controls it, killed it stone dead, then pushes it forward on his right foot. Denis Smith was only a couple of yards away from him and, believe me, Denis would throw himself at anything. He would break his leg to stop a bloke from shooting. And Denis threw himself at him. George stopped, pulled the ball around Denis with his right foot and left him stranded. Alan Bloor then comes in to tackle him. George now lifts the ball with his left foot – same thing. Alan goes to block and suddenly George pulls it back round on his right foot. Alan is left stranded and George is now in the penalty spot position. There's nobody on him. I come off my line. He sees me coming, dummies me, throws me completely the wrong way, pulls the ball around me and rolls it over the blooming line. What a bloody goal! Ah! An absolutely magnificent goal this one – absolutely fantastic! It really was. Fabulous goal.

Did he say anything to you when he scored?
"Pick that out Banksy!" He was a bugger was George, a little sod! [Laughter.] A great player, terrific player; it's just a real shame why he retired early in his career. He spoiled a lot of people's pleasure because he used to fill a ground. They literally would come to see George Best play. The grounds would be sold out and they just wanted to see him play; he was such a great performer. So he spoiled it for them by retiring early. Then, of course, he became an alcoholic, which is so tragic as it made him very very ill. Many people are sad that it worked out for him like it did.

I remember telling him a joke before an England v Ireland International after lining up for the national anthem. Just as the players would be running to each half to knock the ball about I remember calling, "George, come here. Have you heard this one?" [Laugher]. Seriously! And he'd run off laughing before the game.

Oh! We had a lot of fun. A smashing bloke – I liked him – a great chap.

What about Jimmy Greaves?
Greavesy. Ah! Terrific player. A little bit similar style of play to George actually. Jimmy was a poacher in the box and he scored nearly all his goals doing what George did, which was pretending to shoot or calmly pushing the ball into the corner of the net. When he was under pressure, he could push the ball past the defender who was blocking the view of the goalkeeper and shove it into the corner of the net.

Cheeky little players but – my goodness – great great finishers. Terrific finishers. He scored a lot of really good goals. Very clever goals.

The 1966 World Cup was sad for him, wasn't it? No substitutes allowed then, so he missed the knockout stages, including the final.
That's right. Once he got injured against France in the final group game, he came out of the team and Geoff Hurst got in. Jimmy hadn't scored in any of the three games. For the Quarter Final, Alf made some changes. Geoff came in and scored the winning goal against Argentina. We still weren't conceding and were doing fairly well. So, Alf decided to

stick with Geoff and Jim couldn't get back in. That was the only reason.

Did you ever play against Sir Stanley Matthews?

I did on one occasion, yes. He was playing for Stoke and I was playing for Leicester at the time. We drew at Filbert Street and we lost against them here in the League Cup. They murdered us because our manager hadn't got a clue about tactics. Stan was nearing fifty at the time and the manager told our left back, "I want you to go wherever Stanley Matthews goes." And, of course, Stan had this done to him so many times in his career that it was a joke. So, all Stan did was run over to his left half position and our bloody bloke follows him, leaving an almighty gap down the middle. They slaughtered us, and I'm thinking to myself, 'That's great tactics that.' After the first fifteen or twenty minutes, as a manager, you'd be thinking, 'I can't have this; I've got to close the gap.' But no! He never did it. Oh, dear!

What about Terry Conroy? Terry seems to be a legend around Stoke as well?

Yes. Terry did ever so well when he came. He did a super job. He scored a lot of the important goals. A good centre forward; yeah, a good player. He worked hard in training. And, again, this thing in the dressing room; we had a lot of the lads take the mickey out of one another and Terry was great at that. We all joined in. You had the odd one or two, but even they had to succumb to it. They had to join in finally. [Laughter.]

I spoke to Terry one day about the League Cup Final and the goal he scored. He said, "I look back now on those days and it's like a dream. It's almost like it's not me, like it's another person."

Another person, oh ah! I could be wrong, but I'm sure it was the only Cup Final he played in. And to actually be there – to see the people of Stoke in Wembley Stadium – for the first time in over 100 years was wonderful. They were absolutely ape, just delighted to be there. They thought we were going to lose because Chelsea had such a good season and they were the favourites to win. The people had gone to Wembley to have a super day. But then, to win – they went bloody mad! When we got back here you should have seen the reception the team got. Fantastic! It really was.

One thing sticks out in my mind upon our return home. We got off the train in Barleston and got an open top bus. We were going through little villages before we got to the actual city. I'll never forget people coming out of their houses and one guy, he obviously must have been a mad supporter, they were lifting him out in a chair because he couldn't walk. Yeah, they were lifting him out in a chair. Oh, it was fabulous, to see all the people thrilled to bits that we got the cup and were showing it to them.

What do you think the game of football has lost from that era?

I think this camaraderie with your fellow players, the friendship, the feeling inside the dressing room. Players today seem to just do their own thing. They come in, they train and then they go home. We used to have lunch together. Maybe three, four or five of us might go off for a sandwich somewhere. George Eastham and I were mad filmgoers. We'd occasionally head off to the cinema together if we weren't training. There was a lovely mix with the rest of the team. George and myself used to go out regularly with our wives after a Saturday game. I'm not sure if that is there with today's players. I think many are very individual people who just want to do what they've got to do – play on a Saturday and go home, and that's it finished.

Do you think big money has destroyed the game?

I think that is one of the reasons they do it. Some of the top players have all the luxuries that they want out of life and are not concerned about their fellow man – they are not concerned about the friends or the people they play with in the team. Perhaps that's unfair, but that's how it seems sometimes. It's just themselves and their families and their home country.

The game has changed as well because the ball is lighter, the pitches are much, much better and they can stroke the ball about; the idea is more of keeping possession today than it was in my day. Back then there was a bit more variation in the game and that, I think, made it a bit more exciting. The pitches would churn up and that would lead to goalmouth scrambles and more excitement again. It's a different game today.

They want goals to go in and I think that's the reason FIFA have made a lighter ball. They're hoping that players can bend this ball and it moves so goalkeepers make mistakes and goals go in. But why don't they then say, 'All right, we'll be a lot fairer here and make sure that every referee, from every corner kick, when an attacking player is trying to get away from his marker and the defender grabs hold of him, has the power to say, 'Penalty!' You must have seen it because it happens in nearly every game and we are being deprived of perfectly good goals. Attacking players are trying to get away to get a clear header at goal. And you would see more goals scored if refs were vigilant and penalised defenders who were unfairly grabbing their opponent from knocking in a perfectly good goal. Why doesn't FIFA insist that refs stop this?

Also, why don't they stop attackers from standing on top of the goalkeeper? He has a right to come out and try to intercept a cross and, equally, if attackers pull his shirt, or grab hold of his arm, they too should be penalised. If those rules were imposed, you would still see goals. So why do they have to put the onus on the goalkeeper to make a mistake to see extra goals? It's nonsense.

But then we're biased Gordon as goalkeepers.
Well, that's right, we have got to stick up for each other. [Laugher.]

What do you think the game needs today?
What do I think it needs? I think it needs to clean its act up with players trying to get other players booked so they can't make another tackle in the game. When they purposely pretend that they have been kicked I really get annoyed. There's so much cheating going on. You see it on television when they give us slow motion replays in every match. They show people cheating and it's only for one reason, to get a player booked so he can't make another tackle. He's

frightened to make another tackle in case he gets sent off. I would like to see that cleaned up and referees being more authoritative with the important parts of football.

I've spoken earlier about some incidents around corner kicks. The other incident is when somebody knocks the ball over the top and it's running out of play. You have the defender behind the ball and an attacker who can reach it; the defender is blatantly obstructing the other player from getting to it, he's allowing the ball to run out for a goal kick. Again, we're being cheated from keeping the ball on the field of play. But the referee never, ever blows for a free kick. It's a blatant obstruction because the forward can get to the ball before it rolls over the line. He's got there and he can play it, so why shouldn't the defender be made play the ball as well? If he obstructs, then a free kick should be awarded against him. They never, ever blow for it.

If it was made an offence to shield the ball by obstructing the attacker, the defender would then be forced to play the ball back to the goalkeeper or he would have to perform some trick – spin round, whatever. But he cannot obstruct the player from getting to the ball. Things like that I would like to see changed.

And what about the fact that a footballer's career is so short? Men like you, for example, must look at young guys now who earn in a year what you earned in a lifetime.

My opinion about the money that's given to players today is that we have to say it's too much and for one reason. The smaller clubs are struggling like mad to survive and they are the foundations of the league. It starts with these – then it goes up to the pinnacle. If the smaller clubs start to crumble, then everything will crumble. Many of these clubs are literally surviving on a shoestring. So, unless these people can keep going, we are in danger of weakening the very foundation upon which the entire structure depends.

My old club Leicester City had to get a conglomerate of so many people to keep it going. Here, at Stoke City, there is a conglomerate of 16 Icelandic people – all chipping in. But they don't have an endless supply of money. If it crumbles, if all this money that's coming into the game goes straight out for players wages, then it's going to impact somewhere. We don't know exactly how – yet. But, there is a lot of clubs struggling and a lot in debt.

I have said this for a while: you could halve every player's wages in the Premier League and they'd still be millionaires. They'd still be millionaires! What do they want a lot more money for? I just can't understand why the powers to be are not sitting around a table and considering this. They aren't at the moment. They are just letting it ride and I can't understand that. As I say, it's going to impact somewhere and it's the little people, upon which the entire structure depends, who are suffering.

2006 is the 40th Anniversary of England winning the World Cup. Do you feel nostalgic?

Yes, I feel nostalgic about it. But 40 years is a long time to go without us bringing it back here. I thought we would have won it again before now. We nearly won it in 1990, when we lost to West Germany on penalties in the Semi-Final.

CARL MULLAN: I've really enjoyed listening to everything. The only thing I can say is that, picking up on something you said earlier, when I show my friends the video of the '72 League Cup Final between Stoke City and Chelsea, they're all amazed at how much more enjoyable the game seems to have been. And, it's what you are saying. There was no diving or…

No, that's right.

People just got on…
Got on with the game.

… and it was about playing football…
Yeah!

… for the love of playing football.
Yeah! Yeah!

… and I think that's what it should be about.
Yes, you are correct Carl. I mean, you had your Norman Hunters playing against little George Eastham. George was a terrific player, but he wouldn't want to get hurt and I'd never blame him for that. With Norman Hunter, George would have to know whether he'd have to jump out of the way or not. On the other hand, one of the other lads, like Denis Smith, in a 50/50 ball with Norman would get into that tackle as hard as they could to show him they weren't scared of him. George might not like that kind of combat but, as you say, there was never diving about when they weren't injured. They would just get up and get on with the game. Mostly, in 50/50 situations, whoever was the

stronger one stood up and carried on and the other would get up and start chasing after the ball. It was about getting on with the game. That's right.

Do you have any regrets about your football career?

Regrets? I can't really have any regrets about my football career because I was so fortunate in everything: to find a team to play for, to be there when somebody watched me have a good game, then to have them come again to watch me, and to then enable me to go on to play professional football. So really, I can't have any regrets about football at all. The only regret I have, obviously, is driving that day and, probably being a little bit over zealous, making a mistake. That ended my career as an English professional and international goalkeeper. That's probably the biggest regret.

If you had your life to live over again, would you do anything differently?

Drive better! [Laughter.]

I would love to think I could have gone straight into professional football. But the one thing that made me appreciate the pleasures, the things that I have now, was having to work hard. Having to come through from being very poor to finding the lovely things that can happen to someone who works hard. It was seeing poverty that gave me an appreciation of the better things in life and what I have now. When you can afford to pay for a television, a car and a house, you appreciate it more than if you were born into it. I had to work through being a coal-bagger upon leaving school up to playing for England. When I got there I appreciated the feeling of being better off.

Finally, what would you like to pass on to your children and grandchildren?

I believe that laughter is the greatest therapy anybody can have. I think if you can laugh at a joke, if you can accept somebody taking the mickey out of you and laugh along with it, it's very healthy. I would want my children and grandchildren to be the type of people who would enjoy a joke. To be able to, without being mean, laugh at somebody else's expense, but also be able to have the mickey taken out of them. It's got to work both ways. I think it's great therapy.

I'm sure my dad might have been the one to say to me, "You never know what road life is going to take you on." It doesn't just stay all in one direction, it twists and turns and you never know which direction it's going to go. You have to take the rough with the smooth. You have to laugh at adversity. You've got to say, "Right, that's past, that part has gone, let's think of something nice and pleasant because the bad ones are always going to come in life and if you can do someone a good turn then do it."

That's what my kids and grandkids should learn.

So, after all that, who is Gordon Banks?

Who is Gordon Banks? Gordon Banks is a man who, through a little bit of fortune, a little bit of luck, went on to work very hard to establish himself as a goalkeeper, who went on to play for England in the World Cup in 1966 and enjoyed every minute of it.

Gordon Banks: At a Glance

Born: 30 December 1937 (Sheffield, England)

Teams:
1948-52 Tinsley County School and Sheffield Boys
1953-55 Millspaugh Steelworks and Rawmarsh Welfare
1957-58 Royal Signals (National Service)
1955-59 Chesterfield
1959-67 Leicester City
1967-72 Stoke City
1977-78 Fort Lauderdale Strikers

International debut: 1963 v Scotland

English Club Appearances:
Chesterfield	26
Leicester City	356
Stoke City	246
Total:	**628**

England Appearances:
Under-23	2
Full-International	73

'Banks of England' kept a clean sheet in 35 of his 73 appearances for England. Until he was beaten by a Eusebio penalty in the Semi-Final of the 1966 World Cup Finals, he had kept seven clean sheets in a row (an England record). Pelé said of Banks: "For me, Banks was the leading goalkeeper of the 1970 games and, quite possibly, the leading defender in any position. The best in the world."

Last English League Appearance: Liverpool v Stoke City, 21 October 1972

Last England Appearance: Scotland v England, 27 May 1972

Honours:
1956: FA Youth Cup runners-up (Chesterfield)
1957: Rhine Cup Winner (Royal Signals)
1961: FA Cup runner-up (Leicester City)
1963: FA Cup runner-up (Leicester City)
1964: League Cup Winner (Leicester City)
1965: League Cup runner-up (Leicester City)
1966: World Cup Winner
1972: League Cup Winner (Stoke City); Footballer of the Year; Subject of Eamon Andrew's *This Is Your Life*
2000: Honorary President of Stoke City Football Club
2002: Hall of Fame
2006: Honorary Doctorate from Keele University in recognition of his contribution to sport and charitable causes.

FIFA Goalkeeper of the Year: 1966 – 1971

Daily Express Sportsman of the Year: 1971, 1972

NASL Goalkeeper of the Year: 1977

OBE Award: Gordon Banks was awarded the OBE in 1970, two years before his English career was ended by the loss of sight in one eye after a car crash.

Author Acknowledgements

I wish to thank individually and collectively everyone below who, at various times and in various ways, contributed to this story. These include: my late parents, Charles and Sara Mullan; my siblings, Moya, Liam, Cathal and Deirdre; my wife Margaret and our children, Thérèse, Carl and Emma; my neighbours and friends of Leenan Gardens and the people of Creggan, Derry; my teachers at St. Joseph's Secondary School, Creggan, in particular: Mr. Paul Duffy (my favourite); manager of the under-13 team; John Dunne (a modest giant), manager of the under-15 team; Edward and Maureen Armstrong (life-long friends), Conal Byrne (a spellbinding philosopher), Sean Doherty (a wonderful form teacher), Fr. John Irwin (a kind friend), Charlie Fisher (one of the best PE teachers on the planet), Gabriel McDonagh (a gentle man) and Brian Rainey (a wonderful encourager); my team-mates in Leenan Alamo, St. Mary's Boys Club, Creggan Celtic, St. Joseph's Secondary School Under-13 and Under-15 teams and Derry Athletic Football Club; immeasurable gratitude to Jim O'Hea, Derry Athletic's manager and the late Murray Gormley, his assistant; Hillary Carlyle, St. Joseph's under-13 centre forward, for permission to publish the photograph of himself with Pelé and Eusebio; the family of my best friend, the late Shaunie McLaughlin, will always be a second family to me. Sadly, Shaunie's mum and dad and brother Pat have also passed on but an enduring friendship with Maria, Tina, Paul, Jacqueline and Gary survives, and always will; Naomi Wellings, Researcher, BBC Radio; Tim Wedgwood, Presenter, BBC Radio Stoke and Matt Newsum, Broadcast Assistant, BBC Staffordshire Online; Lillian and Malcolm Smith, Ciarán Fadden, Carl Mullan and Aine Kelly for invaluable feedback on the manuscript; Gary Burke, RIP, who departed this life on 7 March 2003; Felix Healy, Jackie Fullerton and Pat Jennings; Annegret Kopp, Mike Kuke-Hartwig and Hans Tilkowski; Bernie Bergin for transcription support; Designers David Houlden and Glen Powell; Seamus Cashman for editorial advice; English sports artist, Alan Damms; sculptor Andrew Edwards; Sr. Anne Walsh and Anthony LaPaglia; Ruth Vitale and her assistant Michael Barlow, my dear friends Richard Moore and Todd Allen for all their encouragement; Patrick and Carmel Walshe; Donal De Roiste; the late Jack Hynes; my brother-in-law, Michael Beatty; Anne Hughes and the Dyslexia Association of Ireland. Also, Mark Redhead and my agent, Elaine Steele.

Thanks to my old friend, Mary Sweeney, her husband Paul Conroy, his brother Mark and their uncle, Terry Conroy, the legendary Stoke City 'Wizard of the Wing'. They too made magic happen. Also to Patrick Loftus. Special gratitude to Bill Flynn of Mutual of America and George Nolan of Nolan Seafoods for making Gordon Banks' visit to Ireland on 3-4 March 2006 possible.

I am forever indebted to Gordon Banks. It was wonderful

to discover that my boyhood hero was, indeed, a worthy role model. Thanks also to his lovely daughter, Wendy, her partner Andy and children, Edward and Daniel. Finally, to my friend Gabriel Byrne who encouraged me to write this story about the influence of Gordon Banks on my life. If I have omitted anyone, it is unintentional and I ask your forgiveness.

For the new edition: Simon Whitehouse for introducing me to Tom Chalmers of Legend Press; Pelé and Archbishop Desmond Tutu for their Foreward. To the Gordon Banks Monument Committee and our 'small' partners who gave me so much support and encouragement in my efforts to raise a fitting monument to the world's greatest goalkeeper: a project that still requires support and must and WILL be completed.

Publisher Acknowledgements

The publisher and editor gratefully acknowledge the permission to quote from: *Banksy* by Gordon Banks (Penguin Books, 2003).

Afterword By Anne Hughes

Hero worship can be dangerous. Idols can have feet of clay. But Don Mullan was wise in his choice of hero. Gordon Banks, when the fourteen-year-old boy first met him in 1970, turned out to be a genuine sportsman, kind and generous with his time. Banks encouraged and advised the shy youngster. No wonder he was inspired to work at his sport, to persevere despite difficulties, and to see the humanity in people of all nationalities.

As a dyslexic child reading was difficult for Don, but he had a good reason to keep at it. He read everything he could lay his hands on about Gordon Banks, and compiled his wonderful scrapbook. The scrapbook that his father showed to Gordon Banks in Ballybofey would never have existed if the youngster hadn't first read the articles and news reports.

It was not until his late 30s that Mullan was diagnosed with dyslexia. For many people, being told that they had a life-long condition, which cannot be cured and which impacts on every aspect of their lives, would be devastating news. For him, as for most people with dyslexia, this diagnosis was not devastating but liberating. It was a great relief to know that there was a reason why he had difficulties at school. Moreover, he learned that he had a high I.Q. This knowledge gave him confidence and encouraged him to undertake projects he would not otherwise have tackled. He went on to write books, make television documentaries, films and engage in investigative journalism.

Now Mullan wants to encourage other people with dyslexia. In telling his own story he emphasises that people with dyslexia can succeed, given the motivation and encouragement.

Don Mullan has said very clearly that he is indebted to Gordon Banks for giving him motivation and self-belief. In this lovely tribute to Gordon, he has amply repaid that debt and, in his turn, provided inspiration to many other people.

Anne Hughes, Director
Dyslexia Association of Ireland

For further information contact:

The Dyslexia Association of Ireland
1 Suffolk Street, Dublin 2, Ireland.
Tel: +353-1-6790276 Fax: +353-1-6790273
Email: info@dyslexia.ie
Website: www.dyslexia.ie

The British Dyslexia Association
98 London Road, Reading RG1 5AU
Helpline Tel: 0118 966 8271
Admin Tel: 0118 966 2677
Fax: 0118 935 1927
Email: admin@bdadyslexia.org.uk
Website: www.bdadyslexia.org.uk

Postscript

The Gordon Banks Monunment

Isn't there a Gordon Banks statue? Didn't Pelé and Archbishop Tutu come to the Britannia Stadium on 12 July 2008 to unveil it? Wasn't it covered by national and worldwide publicity? What has happened to it? Where is it now?

All legitimate questions. For me, they are painful questions too. And I have a lot more of my own.

Our small and dedicated voluntary committee worked very hard, over three years, to create the first monument in the Western World to a goalkeeper – one of the greatest goalkeepers in the history of football and my boyhood hero, Gordon Banks.

Despite the committee's efforts and the generous support of partners such as the Kier Group, Weightmans Solicitors, Bater Tilly International, Sockatyes and the Tollgate Hotel, the three-part monument remains unfinished.

I am currently writing a detailed postscript on the experience. It will describe how our plans, which had been making wonderful progress and gathering much support, were derailed in three short months, leaving me with a large personal debt. It was a disappointing outcome for a project with so much promise, but I retain hope and the story is still unfolding.

A few weeks ago I received a phone call from a friend in England to tell me about the wonderful tribute Derby County Football Club had just unveiled to Brian Clough and Peter Taylor. A monument made by the same sculptor who created the Gordon Banks Monument, Andrew Edwards. My friend said:

> "I wished you could have been present to see how much Derby County Football Club had put into this, at every level, how graciously they had treated their guests, partners and fans, and how hard they must have worked to ensure Brian Clough and Peter Taylor were remembered and celebrated so grandly and appropriately."

It was a different story in Stoke, where support from our two powerful 'partners' – Stoke-on-Trent City Council and Stoke City Football Club – was, at times, detrimental and disappointing respectively.

I encountered two Stokes, though, where I also got to know some of the kindest and most generous people I have met anywhere in the world.

And it is to those kind and generous people that I dedicate this short postscript. For they understand, as Pelé and Archbishop Tutu understand, that at the core of this project was an Irish boy who, as an adult, wanted to honour his English hero, for whom he has retained a lifelong admiration and sense of gratitude. I share their belief that people of goodwill will want this project to be brought to a dignified and appropriate fulfilment.

I have had the privilege of witnessing the esteem with which Gordon Banks is held in both Ireland and the UK. And, I know from my many sojourns to Brazil, that Gordon is, along with Bobby Moore and Bobby Charlton, remembered with immense reverence. Perhaps more so because of 'That Save' from Pelé, which everyone recalls and which is now being used in a powerful advertisement on Brazilian television to promote Pelé's 'Goals for Life' campaign, helping sick children in Brazil and around the world.

Indeed, one of the most positive outcomes is an extraordinary involvement, for me personally, in working closely with Pelé in creating partnerships with the Pelé Little Prince Hospital Research Complex, Brazil, and children's hospitals throughout Europe. There is also the Desmond and Leah Tutu Peace Choirs that I am developing worldwide, and which have their seeds in a wonderful encounter at the King's Hall, Stoke, between Archbishop Tutu and Nottinghamshire's 'Choir Invisible'.

As of now (and I apologise to my follow Stoke City fans for this) I would prefer the Gordon Banks statue to go to Sheffield FC, the oldest football club in the world, whose chairman, Richard Tims, has expressed a desire to acquire it, including finding a £30,000 sponsor, the monies of which will go towards six charities my committee still have a responsibility to. The city of Sheffield is, of course, the birthplace of Gordon Banks and, therefore, an entirely appropriate home.

Have I failed? In the eyes of some perhaps. Yet I see so many positives to be built upon. I am reminded of the words spoken by Lucio in Shakespeare's *Measure for Measure*: 'Our doubts are our traitors, and make us lose the good we oft might win, by fearing to attempt.'

I remember as a boy standing on the Antrim coast with my father, looking across at Rathlin Island. He told me the tale of Scottish King, Robert the Bruce, who, having suffered several defeats in battle is thought to have taken refuge in a cave there. One day, feeling despondent and dejected, he watched a spider make several attempts to spin a web, only to have its efforts destroyed by a strong wind. Undeterred, the spider kept trying until it eventually succeeded. And then my father told me the inspirational quote that gave Robert the Bruce the courage to return to Scotland and rally his troops to victory: If at first you don't succeed – try, try and try again.

Try again, I will. And I'm certain the Gordon Banks Monument Project will ultimately succeed!

Don Mullan
Dublin, Ireland
1 September 2010